TO: _____

FROM: _____

DATE: _____

A *Godly* Home

HOW TO BUILD RELATIONSHIPS IN EVERY ROOM

Hattie R. Butts

WESTBOW
PRESS
A DIVISION OF THOMAS NELSON

WestBow Press books may be ordered through booksellers or by contacting:

WestBow Press
A Division of Thomas Nelson
1663 Liberty Drive
Bloomington, IN 47403
www.westbowpress.com
1-(866) 928-1240

ISBN: 978-1-4497-7051-8 (sc)
ISBN: 978-1-4497-7049-5 (hc)
ISBN: 978-1-4497-7050-1 (e)

Library of Congress Control Number: 2012918966

Printed in the United States of America

WestBow Press rev. date: 10/16/2012

To my daughter, Daphne Butts Tracey
my granddaughters, London Pearl Ruth
and Sariyah Grace
my sisters Gertrude and Ernestine
Julia, my best friend and my encourager

And to godly homes being built

Contents

Acknowledgments ix

Introduction xi

Chapter 1 Entry: A Greeting of Gratitude. 1

Chapter 2 Living Room: You're Invited 15

Chapter 3 Dining Room: Please! Wait to Be Seated . 29

Chapter 4 Kitchen: Family Matters. 47

Chapter 5 Bathroom: A Scent of Self-Worth 65

Chapter 6 Bedroom: Relationships 81

Conclusion. 103

Confessions 109

Appendix. 119

Conclusion. 145

Acknowledgments

My deep appreciation goes to those who have help me accomplish this dream:

Leon, my wonderful, supportive husband of thirty-eight years; my son Derrell, who deposited words of encouragement weekly; my daughter Daphne, who prayed for me daily and who reminded me of the dream that has been locked inside of me; Derrick, my younger son, who helped me get started by coming twice a week to type for me and who inspired me to do what God has spoken to me; Gertrude Horne, Ernestine Pellum, Julia Chambers, Pastor Deanna Andrews, Tina Mitchell, Delessa Haynes, Deborah Jackson, Lisa Singleton Greene, Edna Davis, Joyce Williams, Jewel Edward, Carolyn Powell Wade, Myra Douglas, Marilyn Hill, Nanette LeDuc, Annie Skinner,

Marion Bedell, Pamela Quinney, Lola Williams, Leslie Joe, Rebecca Pollock, Phil McLarty, my spiritual growth class, the ladies at the beauty shop, and Sean C. Wright for critiquing this manuscript.

A special thanks to Opal Rendon for sharing Christ with my entire family and being a godly woman in word and deed. To Marilyn Burke: thank you for praying with me and for teaching me how to live for God in my home and how to be a successful homemaker. To Claudia Whiddon: thank you for giving me a book in Guam that inspired me to live for God and to become a successful homemaker.

And to those who have been praying for me, near and far: thank you, all.

Introduction

Greetings, dear reader!
I offer you six chapters of advice on how to honor the Lord in every room of your home and how to fulfill God's assignment to us as women of God.

You will discover how to be your happiest with the family God gave you.

You will learn how to bring God's limitless and eternal love into your home.

You will get tips on how to be the best you can be—as a wife, mother, and friend.

The concept for this book started out innocently enough. I worked in a model home for ten years, and let me tell you, people were oh-so-excited about seeing a house that would potentially be theirs one day. Some were not even in the real estate market; they just came to see floor plans and to check out the latest furniture and amenities. Some came by just to get decorating ideas for their current houses. As they went from room to room in the model home, they speculated about what furniture would fit best in each room, what color the walls would be, and what room each child would have.

It slowly began to sink in that God wanted me to write a book about the homemaking process. But I was hesitant, going back and forth about it. *Lord*, I asked him, *do You really want me to write this book? Speak, Lord, for your daughter is listening.* I am a person who has faith and courage to step outside the box and *do* what God wants me to do, as long as I believe it is from God. But the project seemed nearly impossible to conquer. You can plainly see, godly women, that God always helps us do what He calls us to do. It's an overused phrase, but it's so true: with God, all things are possible!

It's not news that a home is a place where people live. Without people, it's merely a structure: concrete, nails, shingles, and boards. When a new housing development goes up, the builders build two or three model homes for potential home buyers to see new floor plans, the finest décor, the latest trends, the newest colors, the finest upgrades, and beautiful landscaping. Everything in the house is dressed to the nines! People openly drool over these big, expensive versions of dollhouses. They dream of having such homes where they can be queens or kings of suburbia.

I realized that the model home was but a placeholder; it was pretty, but it was empty. Every day I was there, I would put up a sign in the morning that said *Open*. At the end of the day, the sign said *Closed*. Yes, these models were gorgeous, beautiful, striking … you get the idea. But they had no heart and soul, no intimate relationships, and no traditions. Unfortunately, many of us can identify with the Model Home Syndrome: the outside is beautiful—"designer wallpaper, perfect moldings and finishes, cute décor, and expensive furnishings."

—but the inside is as hollow as a drum. There may be people "living there," but it still feels empty, because your relationships are not the best and sometimes you feel like an imposter.

We all want that ideal home filled with love, laughter, and a husband who loves us. But we often believe that we can achieve those goals with material things. This mentality starts early. Remember when we were young girls who begged our parents to buy us some big, shiny, awesome toy? Do you remember what happened afterward? We often played with it for about two weeks before getting bored with it, and then it ended up at the bottom of the toy box. Then the process started all over again with another toy. As we grew, our toys got more expensive, but the situations didn't change: we were still hoping that something tangible would make us happy.

It's time to grow up, ladies! Completely! The only way to acquire a loving home and positive relationships is to invite God in. There are no shortcuts: No more looking for love in all the wrong places, as the song goes. No more doing the wrong things and associating with the wrong people. Stop looking around you. Instead, allow God to direct your life and to order your steps. He knows exactly how to do this. He knows where you live, He knows your address, and He is indeed able to bring it to pass. Just trust him! He has designed your destiny and knows what is best for you.

Kudos to you, sister, for taking the first step in making Christ your priority! Instituting a godly home is not easy. Just as a bird builds a nest, it is done stick by stick. It takes remarkable patience and commitment. And we all know that any sturdy structure has a good foundation. Think of the Holy Spirit as an architect who drew the original plans for your home and family. In order to keep your relationships strong, the foundation must be strong. That strength comes from God. He can remodel anything. All those that let Him enter their homes are truly blessed. So, dear reader, let's get to building!

Chapter 1

Entry: A Greeting of Gratitude

Develop an attitude of gratitude, and give thanks for
everything that happens to you, knowing that every step
forward is a step toward achieving something
bigger and better than your current situation.
—Brian Tracey

Congratulations on taking the first step in making a positive change in your life! You could desire anything from a wide range of goals: finding a mate, getting gainfully employed, finishing your degree, eliminating debt, finding spiritual peace, or improving relationships. Whatever it is you seek in order to be content, you have the power within you to obtain it.

Even though the goals listed above can act as catalysts for personal happiness, one has to eventually question how long this happiness will remain. This never-ending ebb and flow of happiness is comparable to filling a balloon with air over-and-over, only to have it repeatedly deflate. You can keep refilling it, but the balloon will eventually give out. Talk about frustrating! God did not intend for His children to be worn-out balloons. Therefore, as godly women, we must seek joy that keeps us spiritually inflated on a regular basis.

Before I share my philosophy with you, I would first like to share my journey.

When I was a younger woman, I wanted things to happen *to* me or *for* me to make me happy. For example, I recall that in my twenties I lived for a compliment from my husband. I would go out and buy a new dress, but my smile only came after he remarked on how good I looked. In my thirties, I wasn't happy until our bank account grew, or our home was built, or we acquired other material things.

With age comes wisdom, as they say. It wasn't until my forties that I got my "aha moment," realizing that happiness is short-lived if you depend on external factors—other people and things—to create it. From that moment on, the equation was simple:

happiness inside = happiness outside

This realization gave me a fresh perspective of God's Word. Nehemiah 8:10 states, "The joy of the Lord is your strength." It's only one sentence, but it has more than one valuable lesson:

1. God wants us to have joy.
2. God wants us to be strong.
3. Our Lord brings joy to those who put their faith in Him.

We often spend our lives running like hamsters on one of those wheels—lots of spinning without ever getting anyplace. This easily becomes a pattern in our lives, and we don't realize that we are looking to other people or things to be the pot of gold at the end of the rainbow.

I was weary of the peaks and valleys of that lifestyle, and I wanted the cycle to end. I began to surround myself with people who were not hamsters, so to speak. I befriended a special lady named Opal.

My doorbell rang each day, and I knew it was my best friend, Opal. How did I know? Opal had a distinct habit of ringing the doorbell twice and following it with a single knock. My entire family knew who it was, and someone would shout, "Ms. Opal is here!" We all loved Opal—except my husband, Leon. Leon didn't dislike her, but he just couldn't figure out why this lady came to our home each day and why was she always so happy. At the time, my husband didn't know the Lord, so he thought Opal was annoyingly perky when, in fact, she was truly joyful. People often confuse happiness and joy, but there is a world of difference. Happiness is predicated upon what happens in our lives. Joy is that sincere peace within that radiates outward to touch others. Opal had the latter, as well as an infectious, radiant smile that one just could not help but return.

Ms. Opal truly lived up to the dazzling jewel of her name. She always had a kind word for everyone in my home, and she specifically sought out my husband to speak to him. She wanted God's best for my family, including Leon. It almost seemed a daily mission for her to seek him out and speak to him, even if his reply was less than pleasant.

"How are you doing today, Leon?" Opal would ask.

"Fine. Why do you always ask me that?" he'd reply.

Initially, Leon just could not figure out why this lady would make it a point to seek him out and inquire about his well-being. After all, it wasn't as if they were close. So why should she care? But Opal's joy was earnest too. She spoke to him every time she visited. Over time, my husband came to realize that Opal was sharing God's love with everyone; it didn't matter if you were her bosom buddy or merely an acquaintance. Everyone was under one umbrella in Opal's world.

Opal's cheerful disposition is explained in Proverbs 18:24 (NKJV), which says, "A man who has friends must himself be friendly." Opal didn't wait on someone to befriend her first. Instead, she seized the initiative and ensured that she was always friendly and helpful to whomever she encountered. Inevitably, this led to her having many friends, simply because folks could so easily recognize Opal's own friendliness, which encouraged them to reciprocate her kindness. Opal's greetings of gratitude—greetings that showed others she was thankful to be in their company—served as her invitation to have a deeper conversation filled with meaning and purpose.

First impressions are always important. What better place to make a good first impression than at one's front door? It's the perfect opportunity to immediately set the tone for future interactions with people who come to your home.

Think about someone who is currently an important part of your life, and remember back to the time when you first met him or her. Human nature would indicate that you most likely made an almost immediate assessment of them based on your first impression. I would even go so far as to say that portions of your first impression remain to this day.

I like to consider Opal's ringing of my doorbell as an announcement of something wonderful. I'm sure you've heard of opportunity knocking. A knock at the door notifies us that this is our chance to greet someone and make a good first impression. It could be a family member, a neighbor, a solicitor, or an enemy disguised as a friend.

Regardless of who it is, we as godly women have a moral responsibility to maintain gratitude toward anyone who comes to the front door. Even if it happens to be someone I may not wish to converse with at that time, it is still my responsibility to maintain a sense of gratitude and to discover the reason for his or her visit. God evidently wanted me to cross paths with these people; therefore, I am obligated to see what joy I can bring to their lives.

I now realize that, every day, God gives me not only the opportunity but the responsibility to positively affect the lives of all who set foot in my house. My outlook may well set the tone for the rest of that person's day—and possibly even beyond that. I came to understand that God wanted me to honor Him with my home, so I made it a point to greet every guest with three things: a smile, a positive word, and an appropriate touch.

Smile

Did you know that it takes more muscles to frown than it does to smile? Seriously, think about occasions when someone greets you, especially when you arrive at his or her home. Doesn't a warm smile make all the difference? It makes you feel welcome. Clearly, they want you to visit, and they are happy to see you. A smile can also lift a person's spirits. What a privilege it is to do something powerful and wonderful—all with the simplicity of a smile!

A Positive Word

Many people don't realize the power of kind words. It can be something as simple as a sincere "good morning." There have been times when I've been down in the dumps, and then my mood immediately brightened because of a cheerful word or two. Being genuine when smiling and offering upbeat words can make a world of difference in people's lives.

Another benefit to making complimentary statements is the gateway it opens into meaningful conversation. It allows your visitors to feel relaxed, especially if they are first-time visitors. Remember, your words should always encourage, edify, and empower. The Word of God tells us that if we truly are one of the Lord's disciples, part of our duty and obligation to Him is to sustain those who are weary with a "word." Keep the words of Isaiah 50:4 close to your heart: "The Lord GOD has given Me the tongue of disciples, that

I may know how to sustain the weary one with a word. He awakens Me morning by morning, He awakens My ear to listen as a disciple."

An Appropriate Touch

It is difficult to judge what exactly is or is not appropriate physical contact when greeting someone. A good rule of thumb is to maintain eye contact and offer to shake the visitor's hand. This assures visitors that they are in a welcoming environment and that they should feel as though they are amongst friends. People are touchy about giving hugs and the like when first meeting, but a good, warm handshake is an excellent icebreaker.

If you know the visitor well, a brief hug upon entering may be appropriate instead of a handshake. Make sure that your intention is clearly meant just to be friendly, and never hug a person whom you know has an aversion to such gestures or gets squeamish when it comes to physical contact. But in most circumstances, a hug with a little pat on the back is very much appreciated. It's a wonderful signal that people who come to your home will be treated like family, and it serves as a powerful token of your hospitality.

Wrap Up

In addition to the above practical points, there are numerous spiritual lessons to be learned by reflecting on the role of gratitude in our lives and in our homes. Here are just a few:

1. *Have a morning gratitude session.* Every day that the Lord grants to you in this life is a new opportunity to advance the cause of His kingdom. Take one minute in the morning—make it a daily ritual—to just spend some time with Jesus and let Him know how thankful you are for all of the blessings in your life. It will help to keep you in a grateful frame of mind the whole day through.

"This is the day which the LORD has made; Let us rejoice and be glad in it" (Psalm 118:24).

2. *Make a gratitude list when life's ride is bumpy.* Stressed out from work? Got into an argument with somebody? Received bad medical or financial news? Any of these things and lots of others can really add up to an awful day. Yet in the midst of it, God is still there! Instead of dwelling on the troubling aspects of your life, make a list of all those many positive things that enrich your life and bring you happiness. In all likelihood, it will be a much longer list than whatever it is that is stressing you out.

"In everything give thanks; for this is God's will for you in Christ Jesus" (1 Thessalonians 5:18).

3. *Be grateful for your children.* If you have kids, you know what a challenge they can be, especially when they are very young or in their teen years—and in some cases, even into adulthood! But can you imagine life without them? Children are one of the sweetest blessings that our Lord bestows on us. So the next time they are driving you crazy and making you want to yank your hair out, recall and reflect on all the joy they have brought you—the time they declared you their hero or made you laugh at the end of a rough day. Thank God for the gift of children that He has so graciously given to you.

"Do everything without complaining or arguing" (Philippians 2:14 NLT).

4. *See the glass as half full.* Appreciate what you *do* have, my friend. It's terribly easy to focus on what we *don't* have, but that is not God's way. Instead, He wants us to be grateful for all that we *do* have, and indeed we should give Him thanks for literally everything. He sustains all of our needs throughout our entire lives. How could we possibly not be grateful for that?

O LORD, you are my God; I will exalt You, I will give thanks to Your name; for You have worked wonders, plans formed long ago, with perfect faithfulness. (Isaiah 25:1).

The Entrance to Your Home

All of these points are vital in making a person feel welcome when visiting your home, but there are other things that you as a godly woman can do to make sure the entrance to your home gives the initial impression of being a warm, inviting space. Following are some ways to allow the entrance to your domain to be inviting to all who visit.

Outdoor Furniture

If you have a large entryway, porch, or patio, what could be more inviting than some comfortable chairs—maybe rocking chairs—and a small table? This conveys to visitors the idea that this is a home where people can stay and visit without fear of invading the homeowner's space. It says that they are welcome to sit down, have a cool drink, and visit for as long as they like. The table is also a means of serving snacks or engaging in a game or other types of fellowship, which are all important aspects of hospitality.

Welcome Mat Style

A front mat does not necessarily have to say "Welcome" in order to get the point across to visitors. A front mat should be a reflection of the family's overall personality. Some prefer to have their names on the mats, while others like to have cute little puppies or kittens on them. Whatever the style, this personal touch speaks volumes to visitors.

Bright Lights

When people visit your house after sunset, what kind of lighting do you have? If it is dark and dimly lit, casting long shadows into every corner, that wouldn't be very inviting, now, would it? If that's the case, make an investment in new lighting fixtures that brighten your home and lighten the mood. It doesn't have to be anything fancy or expensive, just the kind of lighting that sets a cheerful ambiance for the outer entrance to your home.

Clean Glass

One of the characteristics we women notice when visiting other people's homes is attention to detail—or lack thereof. Naturally, as you approach a person's entrance, you notice whether or not the glass on their front door and windows is clean. Clean glass shows visitors that you care about the minute details of your home. It may seem trivial, but a polished home sends the message that visitors will receive undivided attention too!

My Homework Assignment for Chapter 1

1.

2.

3.

4.

5.

6.

Chapter 2

Living Room: You're Invited

The time to relax is when you don't have time for it.
—Sidney J. Harris

Sometimes the most important thing in a whole day
is the rest we take between two deep breaths
or the turning inwards in prayer for five short minutes.
—Etty Hillesum

Hello again! If you are reading this, it means you are still with me and are sincere about letting the light into your life and home. I'm so glad you are staying with me! The objective of this chapter is to stress the importance of how our living rooms reflect our attitude toward the Lord and toward being a witness. Once again, I look to my dear friend Opal as an example. Her sunshine didn't just stop at the foyer; it spilled into every room.

"Hattie, I love the wreath on your front door. Is that new?" she asked on her first visit to my home.

"Yes it is, Opal. I've been working on it for a week now, and I finally finished it."

Opal would later notice everything on her daily visits—even brief ones. This time she noticed my wreath and welcome mat while on the porch before she entered the door. Gosh, Ms. Opal even complimented me on how pretty my front-door locks were. Once inside, she took note of the candles that I had near the entrance of my home.

"Come on in, Opal," I said, and she continued into the living room.

"Hattie, you have such a pretty living room. It's so orderly. Do the kids live here during the week?" she asked, half-joking.

"Why do you say that?" I asked, chuckling.

"Because," Opal stated, "I don't see any toys, shoes, or clothes around. It is extremely neat."

Growing up in the sticks of Florida, my parents, early on, instilled in me and my siblings the importance of maintaining on our own living space. They said, "Your home should be a witness to your family, friend, or whoever God sends." Our parents taught us to love our home, no matter whether it was a shack or a castle, because everything we have belongs to the Lord. Later on, I realized that homes have purpose beyond keeping a roof over our heads. They are to bring joy to you and your visitors. You should be happy while you live there, doing your best to get the highest resale value.

Anyway, Ms. Opal and I continued to the living room. I didn't keep her from this room, even though I just was a little funny about people roaming my space. When we reached my living room, Opal went straight to my sofa and sat. After I joined her on the couch, she told me about her family, and I shared a little about mine.

That day was the beginning of many visits from Ms. Opal. Some were fine, and some were a little offbeat. You see, Opal was bold. She wouldn't hesitate to ask questions that many people might feel weren't any of her business. She'd ask me outright where my husband was. But then she'd come by with gifts for my children, even after I'd told her over the phone that we didn't need anything. My friend and I shared laughter and tears in my living room. Sometimes our conversations on my couch were light and breezy. Sometimes they were stern, like when I confided in her about some family problems.

The point I am making with this Opal story is this: keeping a well-organized, attractive living area serves as a nest that nurtures relationships.

It was in the comfort of my cozy home that Opal shared her philosophy with me, which I, in turn, am sharing with you. She embraced Christ and was a witness for Him. Opal reminded me of how Jesus had died on the cross for all of our sins, hers and mine. All I had to do was invite him in—the same way I had invited Opal into my home—and he would forgive my sins and help me through my family issues or any other problems.

Opal demonstrated Jesus' love, and I became very interested in what she was saying. She read the Bible to me when she came over, and we prayed about finding solutions to my family issues. Slowly but surely, my family relationships improved. As time passed, Ms. Opal took my children along to Bible study once a week with her son. My children began to know the Lord too, and their lives changed for the better right before my very eyes. Opal's joy gave way to love for us, and I was grateful to her commitment to my family.

So I ask you this: is your house a home? If you have work to do in this area, start by knowing that God's purpose for homes is to reflect Him in every room with the message of hope, love, and acceptance. When we build our homes, we want to keep Christ in mind first, because He is the one who initially provided it for us. He is our source. We Christians are often encouraged to be good stewards. What does that really mean? The simple definition of a steward is "someone who's trusted with another's goods." Everything we have belonged to God first and still does. With that in mind, we should immediately rid ourselves of attitudes like: "It's mine; I can wreck it if I want to." We simply hold our earthly goods in trust for Him.

This should free us from slavery to *our* material things. God may do what He wishes with *His* things. So why be concerned about the possibility of losing everything?

This doesn't mean that we neglect what God allows us to steward. The Bible states in so many words that if we do well with what we've got, we'll be rewarded with more. In other words, having little is no excuse for not taking care of what we've got. Peter writes that God provides all that is necessary and indispensable to life. An abundant life is ours through a relationship with God and through practicing godliness. Godliness means living with God-like qualities or simply demonstrating God's word in our actions. Of course, as imperfect humans, it becomes obvious that we must find the power source to live in a godly way, even through trials. This ties in to what I said in the previous chapter about seeing the glass as half-full. When life throws you a curve ball, you only have to look around to find something to smile about. There is never a shortage of sunny days, a friend who makes you laugh, or a big slice of your favorite cake.

God says, "Delight yourself in the LORD; and He will give you the desires of your heart" (Psalm 37:4).

"Hope deferred makes the heart sick, but desire fulfilled is a tree of life" (Proverbs 13:12).

The "living room" of your heart and mind must be cleared and redecorated with these thoughts first:

- *Handle things with care.* After all, they don't belong to you. They were temporarily loaned to you, so use them with respect.
- *Be generous.* Our God wants us to do his work by blessing others with gifts whenever possible. It could be a ride to work or babysitting on the spur of the moment.
- *Be fruitful.* This implies producing rather than consuming. Or this could be interpreted as leaving something in better condition than you found it.
- *Know when enough is enough.* We get into trouble when we want things we can't afford and even things we can afford. God says plainly that where your treasure is, there your heart will be also (Matthew 6:21).

Today, your loving Father is calling you to a personal relationship with Him. Let go of all things that will hinder your personal relationship with God, and allow Him to equip you with all you need to live a godly, abundant life.

Once you know the Lord in your heart and mind, it's time to bring Him into your living quarters. This could be a pleasant experience for everyone in the family. My parents may not have had the biggest home on the block, but our home would be voted as the best-kept home on the block. How did our home receive top ratings? It took work—hard work—from everyone.

There were four girls and my baby brother, and my parents had a job for each of us. We mopped, vacuumed, washed dishes, did laundry, cooked, and kept our own rooms neat. When we were growing up, our family observed spring cleaning like a time-honored ritual. It was different from regular housekeeping in that we first made an all-out assault on a year's worth of filth and clutter. Once the house was cleared of unwanted things, we focused on deeper attention to detail. We waxed the hardwood floors, washed the windows inside and out, and hung the blankets, quilts, and comforters out to be refreshed by the warm sunlight and spring breezes.

It wasn't always fun for us children to do this, as it was usually done on a Saturday, but we did our best, and the benefits were immeasurable. No matter how much we may have harped over the imposition of it all, we swelled with pride as we breathed in the sweet scent of fresh wax, furniture polish, and disinfectant that filled our home with a spring-like freshness. I have somewhat carried over that tradition into my own family in order to create a godly home, and I am sharing that with you. Try to look at your living room from a visitor's point of view.

Wrap Up

Are you surrounded by clutter in every room in your home? Clutter is visually distracting and stressful. Every item you see demands yours mind's attention, and no matter how short that attention is, and despite it's being subconscious, these little distractions add up. It's difficult to have peace or to focus amid this clutter. Add to this the wasted time and energy needed to look for things, to maintain things, and to clean things, and you will notice that the more clutter you have, the more energy it will take.

I recommend that you focus on one room of your house per week until you have de-cluttered your home and made it a peaceful and calming place to be. Don't try to do your whole house at once, as this can be very overwhelming and time-consuming—unless you just have a lot of time on your hands, in which case, go for it! Focus on clearing out one room of unused items, and try to work at it fifteen minutes a day, unless you get carried away and feel like doing more. Skip the closets and drawers for now. We'll tackle those later. Focus now on the things you can immediately see.

- *Start big.* Is there too much furniture in the room? If so, scale back. Is all of it necessary? Which furniture do you love? Which stuff is just too distracting? Also, consider removing other big items, like boxes full of stuff.

- *Clear all flat surfaces.* This includes desktops, tabletops, countertops, etc. Remove all papers, piles of stuff, and little knickknacks. Put it all on the floor. Now get a trash bag and two boxes. Sort through everything in your piles, one item at a time. Each item should go to one of three places—in the trash bag to be thrown away, in a box of items to give away to friends, family or charity, or in another box of items to be moved to another room in the house.

    Put back only a couple of select items on the flat surfaces, such as a family photo or something that functionally belongs there. But leave the flat surfaces as bare as humanly possible. "Stuff" doesn't belong there. You need to find a drawer, shelf, or container for whatever stuff you've removed. When you're done sorting through the pile, put the recycle box in the trunk of your car and drop it off the next time you go out to do errands. Throw away the trash bag. Take the other box and put the stuff where it belongs elsewhere in the house. But don't put it on flat surfaces unless absolutely necessary!

>   *Repeat this process* for any other "stuff" in the room, including stuff on the floor.

- *Make rounds.* Now move around the room clockwise and clear what's left. This might be stuff on the walls, things posted to surfaces like the refrigerator, items under tables or desks, etc. Leave only what's absolutely necessary. I mostly have blank walls except for a few choice paintings or drawings by my dad, who is an artist. All my flat surfaces are bare. It's nice!

- *Be merciless.* Be a ruthless editor. The more you get rid of, the better!

Okay, your room should look pretty good now. You should feel pretty terrific. Sit down, relax, look around, and enjoy the peace. An organized room has tranquil energy. Savor your triumph.

This editing process is not a destination but an ongoing process. It won't last long if you don't have a system and develop habits to keep it de-cluttered.

Here's the maintenance system that works for me:

- *Choose a place for everything.* This is an oldie, but it's valuable, nonetheless. Are you about to put something down on a flat surface? Stop yourself. Think about where that item belongs. If it doesn't have a home, find one and stick with it. Always put it in that spot. For example: I have a tray for my keys, wallet, etc., and when I first get in the house, I put these things in that tray—every time, so I always know where they are. And when I leave, it's as simple as grabbing my stuff from the tray.

- *Have an inbox for papers.* Create a filing system for important papers, from bills to critical documents to taxes to kids' report cards. Put all incoming mail, school papers, receipts, etc., into that inbox, and process it once a day—or every other day, but not much longer than that. Otherwise you're just creating a piles. When you process, don't leave stuff in a pile to be filed later; file it immediately. Discard other stuff. Pay bills immediately, or put them in a special bills-to-be-paid folder. Don't leave papers lying around.

- *Clean up at night or before you leave.* People say you shouldn't go to bed angry or leave in a huff. The same applies to the condition of your house. Try to leave on a positive note before you turn in or take off. If you've developed good habits, you may not need this tip, but no one's perfect. And if you have kids, you'll definitely need this tip. Just take five to ten minutes to pick up stuff and make sure your flat surfaces are clear.

- *De-clutter like clockwork.* Despite your best efforts, new stuff just accumulates. You need to have a regular purging process. I discard junk every six months to a year.

We don't need a pulpit to share the message of salvation to our family and friends. All we need is to let our light so shine before men, that they may see our good works and glorify our Father in heaven (Matthew 5:16 NKJV).

- *Embrace the light, which is Jesus.* Make the spiritual commitment to have a godly home. Once your internal priorities are straight, working on the external ones are easy.
- *Let God guide.* Once you make the decision to let God into your living space, allow Him to mold and shape you. He has blessed you with what you have, and you must make him proud. Our light is shown through our works (Ephesians 2:8–9 NASB). This also means being generous to others with our time and material things—without limits.
- *Live Godlike.* Our works glorify God. Receive visitors in a clean, well-organized home. Relationships flourish in simplicity and order.

Hopefully, your foyer and living room now reflect your relationship with the Lord and evoke feelings of love, hope, and acceptance to His other children, which are your visitors. Let's move on to another room.

My Homework Assignment for Chapter 2

1.

2.

3.

4.

5.

6.

Chapter 3

Dining Room: Please! Wait to Be Seated

Fill your life with as many moments and experiences of joy and passion as you humanly can. Start with one experience and build on it.
—Marcia Wieder

The best way to pay for a lovely moment is to enjoy it.
—Richard Bach

Come on into the dining room. Let me pull out a chair for you. Have a seat at my well-dressed table while I serve you a big helping of God's Word. Here we nourish our minds as well as our bodies. My friend in Christ, Opal, taught me a thing or two about the dining room as well: the dining room is just as important as the living room for encouraging fellowship.

"Hello there, Hattie. I wanted to invite you and the family over for dinner," Opal stated one day.

"Well," I replied, "I'm sorry, but we can't make it this time. We're busy this weekend. Maybe another time."

Ms. Opal repeated the invitation again and again. She never gave up. Deep down inside, I wished she would leave me alone about it. Don't get me wrong; I loved Opal, but sometimes she was too persistent. And I knew my husband couldn't have cared less about dinner at Opal's. He was already tired of seeing her at our place.

Anyway, my own experience of being invited to dine with someone reminded me of a simple but powerful story I read once:

A woman saw three old men with long, white beards sitting in her front yard. She did not recognize them. She went out to them and said, "I don't know you, but you must be hungry. Please come in and have something to eat."

"Is the man of the house home?" they asked.

"No," she replied. "He's out."

"Then we cannot come in," they replied.

In the evening when her husband came home, she told him what had happened. "Go tell them I am home and invite them in!" he said. The woman went out and invited the men in again.

"We do not go into a house together," they replied.

"Why is that?" she asked.

One of the old men explained, pointing to each of his friends in turn. "His name is Wealth, and he is Success. I am Love." Then he added, "Now go in and discuss with your husband which one of us you want in your home."

The woman went in and told her husband what the man had said. Her husband was overjoyed. "How nice!" he said. "Since that is the case, let us invite Wealth. Let him come and fill our home with wealth!"

The wife disagreed. "My dear, why don't we invite Success?"

Their daughter had been listening from another part of the house. She jumped in with her own suggestion: "Would it not be better to invite Love? Our home will then be filled with love!"

"Let us heed our daughter's advice," said the husband to his wife. "Go out and invite Love to be our guest."

The woman went out and asked the three old men, "Which one of you is Love? Please come in and be our guest." Love got up and started walking toward the house. The other two men also got up and followed him. Surprised, the lady asked Wealth and Success: "I only invited Love. Why are you all coming in?"

The old men replied together: "If you had invited Wealth or Success, the other two of us would've stayed out, but you invited Love, and wherever he goes, we go with him. Wherever there is Love, there also are Wealth and Success!"

I soon realized that Opal's dinner invitations were a form of unconditional love. She was inviting Love in first, just like the story.

"For I was hungry and you gave me something to eat; I was thirsty and you gave me something to drink. I was a stranger and you invited me in" (Matthew 25:35).

In English we tend to use the word *love* casually, almost flippantly, such as when we say, "I love my job" (a rare usage these days) or "I love to watch TV" (all too common). Opal taught me that the Greek word *agape* (ah-gah-pay) could never be used in such situations, because it is *not* found in merely caring for something or someone. *Agape* is an unconditional love for others that is complete—like the love that made our Saviour die for us.

A week later, Opal and her husband invited us to dinner again. My husband and I finally accepted their invitation, and it was a memorable experience—for all the right reasons. I even remember the delicious dinner! We had fried chicken, mashed potatoes, corn, and peas. And the conversation was even better; we came to see just how much we had in common. Our husbands bonded over having been in the military. We compared stories about all the places we had been. They even prayed for us that night.

That pleasant evening reminded me of the Scripture in Acts 2:42–44: "They were continually devoting themselves to the apostles' teaching and to fellowship, to the breaking of bread and to prayer. Everyone kept feeling a sense of awe; and many wonders and signs were taking place through the apostles. And all those who had believed were together and had all things in common."

When my husband was in Opal's part of town for school, she and her husband insisted on having him as a guest. They received my husband with open arms and showed God's love without hesitation, providing food, shelter, and transportation.

Opal and her husband demonstrated boundless hospitality. Shouldn't we all? Shouldn't we always? I'm talking about an open, welcoming, and generous spirit that invites others into our homes and honors their stories. I'm talking about a deep sense of care and concern for others that involves more than serving tasty food. Sometimes the people you invite into your home may look and behave and talk differently from you. That's okay. God's children may not all look the same, but we all feel the same. We all feel hungry and thirsty. And most precious of all, everyone feels overjoyed at someone's dinner invitation.

Hospitality means welcoming the hurting and wounded too, without judgment or malice. We do it by simply standing by and caring for people right where they are. I love the language of the hymn, "Help Us Accept Each Other," which says: "Teach us to care for people—for all, not just for some—to love them as we find them or as they may become." We are to welcome those who are searching for God, without trying to make them like us or forcing them to think like us. For hospitality gives people room to ask questions, to doubt and to find their own way. This is challenging, for sure, but it is nothing to fear. We will be strengthened and renewed by such a challenge!

When we lived in a Dallas suburb in Texas, we attended the Assembly of God church. I remember our pastor asking if we could let another pastor live with us for a week or two. My husband and I said yes. You see, we love people, and our home has always been open to the people God sends. No, this pastor didn't look like us, and yes, he was a stranger, but we served him and he served us.

I can remember him praying for us daily, encouraging us. He had come from New York to serve in the church as a consultant, and he was there to choose a couple who would be overseers to the church elders. He said the Lord had spoken to him about us during prayer. After having observed how we interacted in our home and how faithful we were to each other, he felt that we'd be the ideal couple for the job. My husband and I were overjoyed. Sometimes we don't realize whom we are entertaining!

"Do not neglect to show hospitality to strangers, for by this some have entertained angels without knowing it" (Hebrews 13:2).

Sometimes we have the power to bless others when we receive them. Let me share with you another story about a lady who had an impact on my life. Her husband was abusive, and she had obviously had enough. Our doorbell rang at 3:00 a.m. one morning, and there she was on our porch with her young son, trying to get away from her husband who had beaten her very badly for the umpteenth time. She was covered in blood. My husband immediately got me up from bed, and I cleaned her up and provided help for her son.

She filed charges, and her husband was arrested. My husband was working in the prison ministry at the time and went to talk to the man in jail. I invited her to go to church with me, and she did. Later, she became a member of the same church that I attended. She was already a Christian but was trying to be a godly wife. However, her husband refused Christ. I lost track of the lady for a while.

Ten years passed, and she called me with an update. She told me that her husband had never accepted the Lord and, sadly, had passed away. But she was doing well and attributed it to my husband and me taking her and her son into our home that morning when she'd thought her life was over. We never know whom God will send our way so that we can demonstrate His love and show hospitality to those in need.

"Share with the Lord's people who are in need. Practice hospitality" (Romans 12:13 TNIV).

I will end this chapter with another favorite story about receiving guests.

The Devil had a strong grip on a man; he tormented and oppressed him with no mercy. The man sabotaged everything he did, even driving away his loved ones. He was in survival mode, doing the best he could at his minimum-wage job, barely making ends meet. The man invited his "friends"—Alcohol, Anger, and Pride—to party the sorrows away and help him cope. But it just wasn't working!

After some time had passed without relief, the man thought, "Well, I'll throw a bigger party to numb my pain." So he invited Loneliness, Wrath, Pornography, Shame, and Condemnation; they just mocked and ridiculed him. He was so hopeless that Depression settled in, and he began to contemplate suicide. He wrestled with this, back and forth, not realizing that change was only an invitation away!

Finally, he was sick and tired of being sick and tired. He lifted up his voice and cried out for help. "Jesus, will you come to my house?" Jesus, full of compassion, immediately heard his cry and accepted his invitation.

Jesus said, "You invited me to your house. What do you want me to do?"

The man said, "Save me, Lord. I'm tormented!"

Jesus said, "Show me around your house."

The man, still in tears, proceeded to show Jesus the living room. Behind the couch, they discovered an unclean spirit that was haunting the man. Jesus said, "Do you want the spirit to leave?"

The man replied, "Yes, Lord."

Jesus grabbed the demon and threw it out the front door. They repeated this process in every room, cleansing and kicking out every devil. The man was feeling better and better. He began to see more clearly. Confusion and Anger no longer consumed his thoughts.

Jesus then came to the closet, and the man quickly said, "Oh, no, Lord. Please don't go in there!" Then Jesus went to the basement door, and again, in a panic, the man rushed over and stood in front of Jesus and said, "Don't go down there!"

Jesus was saddened and said, "If you won't let me into every room of your house, I can't totally heal you and set you free."

The man said, "Well, I feel pretty good now. In fact, I feel better than I have in years. Don't be concerned about the closet and the basement, Lord. You have full reign in the rest of my house."

Jesus reluctantly went and sat down on the couch. The man joined him, and as he sat down, there was a knock on the door. The man got up and answered it. The demon rushed in on him, beat him down, and ran into the closet. The man, bleeding and bruised, said, "Jesus, why didn't you help me?"

Jesus answered, "The demon has free access to the closet because you refused to let me in." The man limped over to the closet and said, "Jesus, please help me. Here, you reign over the closet as well." Jesus opened the door with authority and commanded, "Depression, Shame, Pornography, and Escapism—leave!" The demons fled in fear and immediately ran out the front door. The man sighed in relief.

The Lord walked over to the basement door and looked at the man with expectation and eyes of intense fire. The man limped to the door and hung his head low. He said, "Lord, I let you in the closet. Isn't that good enough?" Disappointed, Jesus went and sat back down on the couch. The man joined him.

As they were having a conversation, there was a knock at the door. The man struggled to get up. He walked to the front door and answered it. Seven demons violently thrust themselves into the room, trampling the man underfoot. They kicked and beat him and left him in a bloody mess. After they were through, they scurried into the basement. The man was stunned, barely conscious. Tears filled his eyes as he said, "Jesus, where are you? Help me!"

Jesus rose from the couch and, with tears in His eyes, began to compassionately tend to the man's wounds. Jesus said, "I warned you. You must let me into every room of your house." The man couldn't move, but with a struggling voice he said, "Lord, please deliver me. I give you everything. I give you permission to go into the basement."

Jesus rose and turned toward the basement door. With every step, it was as if hell shook and the devils trembled. Jesus opened the door and, with holy vengeance, commanded, "Pride, Bitterness, Vindication, Rejection, Compromise, Abandonment, and every other devil—leave!" The demons quickly ran out the front door like whipped puppies.

The light in the whole house became brighter! The man was regaining strength as the King of his house spoke with the power of His Word: "Be thou healed." The Lord picked the man up and, with a loving embrace, said, "For you, my son, were dead and are alive again; you were lost and are found." They began to rejoice together, and as they rejoiced, the man's wounds were completely healed.

They went back and sat down on the couch, full of joy. They talked about purpose and destiny. At that time, there was a knock on the door again. The man looked to Jesus with mounting fear. As the man began to rise, Jesus said, "I'm the King of this house. I will answer the door."

Jesus rose majestically with fire in His eyes. He answered the door, and outside was a mob of demons full of revenge and malice. When they saw that the King of Glory had answered the door, they trembled and cried out with one voice, "Oh, we must have the wrong house!" And Jesus commanded them to leave.

The man was grateful as he stood next to Jesus. As the hordes of hell were leaving, the man saw his family in the distance. The man's heart pounded with excitement. As his family came nearer, with every step, the man rejoiced with tears of restoration. He was beside himself as his wife, Faith, and his two daughters, Hope and Love, came to the door. Jesus and the man welcomed them inside with delight. They threw a jubilant party, inviting a new group of friends to celebrate the good things the Lord had done. Jesus greeted every friend at the door.

One after another, He let them in to the party: Kindness, Joy, Liberty, Humility, Peace, Goodness, Mercy, Righteousness, Holiness, Power, Faithfulness, Unity, Self-Control, and Meekness. The man's new friends came in and stayed." (Jeffrey Leonard, Parrott, Jesus is King of this House, Devil Get Out, Kingdom Reality@2008www. ActsInMotion.com)

You are now ready to receive your guests in the beautiful spirit of the Lord. Happy dining, my friends.

Wrap Up

Do you have the gift of hospitality? This little quiz will let you know if you do.

- Do you enjoy having people in your home?
- Do you inconvenience yourself in order to help others?

- Is your home the kind that most people feel comfortable in? Can people drop by to visit unannounced?
- Are you quickly aware of practical needs?
- Do you feel blue when you don't have guests into your home?
- When you view your home, do you see it from the guests' perspective?
- Do you enjoy watching people meet and have fun at parties and events you helped to plan and host?
- Do you consider your home a place of ministry?

If you answered yes to most of these questions, then you naturally have the gift of hospitality and serving. Congratulations! If you don't, do not fret. You may have to work at it, but you can definitely change. Once you commit to making a home more receptive to visitors, you are ready for the fun part: dressing your dining room to evoke a spirit of sharing and relaxation. Let's get started!

Color me friendly.

The color of paint in a dining room can help stimulate or suppress appetites. Warm colors such as orange, red, and yellow are thought to be more appetizing. Blue is generally a soothing, restful color. Blue may not be an appropriate dining-room color simply because there are very few blue foods, so it doesn't have an association with eating. Think of the interior colors of your favorite restaurant when you choose paint colors. If you want a chic or bold dining room, try a gray, brown, or black paint, which will make a big impact for a small price.

Be efficient but stylish.

Dining rooms may be short on space, especially in apartments and condos. You may have just a breakfast nook or part of a living room to use as a dining area. Even if you have very little room for furniture in your dining room, give high style to what you have. Look for furniture that lasts for years to come but also conveys a theme. A formal Queen Anne dining set will give your room an air of elegance. Look for a sturdy oak table with painted legs, if you want a country feel in your eating area.

If you need dining-room furniture on a budget, invest in a staple gun and upholstery fabric to give new life to old chair seats. Paint will instantly transform a used dining table. You can also place a vintage tablecloth over it to disguise flaws. Benches provide ample seating while lending a casual air to the room.

If you have a large dining room and a big table, you may be able to place a small settee on one side of the dining table for a coffeehouse vibe that provides comfortable seating. A buffet can be formal, informal, or retro. Buffets can house china and act as a serving area.

Have fun when choosing a theme for this area. There are no rules or limits!

Accessorize.

Dining room accessories should be both useful and beautiful. For a quick dining room makeover, place shades with fancy feathers or beaded trim on the chandelier. Lamps or lit candles on the buffet provide mood lighting.

Put patterned plates on top of formal chargers for a nontraditional element. Bright plates on the wall showcase your china while giving a French Country feel. You can leave place settings on the table during the day for added sparkle, or transition into table decoration or a centerpiece when the dining room is not in use. You get the idea.

More Tips

Here are some other tips that I have picked up here and there in making over a dining room:

Look to photos. Check out pictures in home-décor magazines or online to get a feel for what you want. Sometimes getting a visual is the best way to get inspired.

Enhance the table. I mentioned above that the table is the focus of the dining room. Remember, it's the most important item in setting the tone for this space. Get a table that offers functionality and reflects the mood you want to create.

Take a seat. Don't forget the chairs to complete your look! Their style should complement the table as well as be comfortable.

Design with high style. If you really want to bring elegance to the dining room, get a chandelier. For a polished look, get curtains or drapes. If you have the space, bring a buffet or sideboard in to store extra dishes, utensils, and napkins. These subtle touches bring effortless sophistication to a dining room.

My Homework Assignment for Chapter 3

1.

2.

3.

4.

5.

6.

Chapter 4

Kitchen: Family Matters

And it is time for those who talk about family values to start valuing families.
—John Kerry

To nourish children and raise them against the odds is, in any time and any place, more valuable than to fix bolts in cars or design nuclear weapons.
—Marilyn French

L et's take a walk into another room of our homes—the kitchen!

The kitchen is where family matters most. It's where families share meals and talk about the day's highs and lows. It's where parents pay bills and kids do homework. It's also a place where parents and kids have opportunities to learn about each other, develop important life skills and family values, and nurture relationships by working together. It's where your mother made her mother's famous cookies, cakes, and pies.

Lately, I have thought seriously about something as simple as the kitchen table and about how, unfortunately, it has lost its place of honor in the modern home. Think back to those old-school TV shows like *Little House on the Prairie* or *The Waltons*. The kitchen table used to hold a prominent place in the home and was where a great deal of action took place. It was often located in front of the fireplace, and it provided a place where family members served meals, did homework, made pies, kneaded bread dough, and read stories. I could go on and on.

Even though those families lived hand-to-mouth, they were rich in love and tradition. Even in TV series set in much later eras, such as *Leave It to Beaver* and *The Andy Griffith Show*, the kitchen table was the activity hub for the house. It was where June Cleaver set out milk and cookies for the boys when they came home from school. Aunt Bea spent a good portion of her time right at her kitchen table, creating more than just food to put on it. She created memories and homemade preserves, and she served tea along with good company.

Sadly, society moved away from this tradition as technology advanced. Nowadays, we eat in front of the TV or even in the car. Gosh, we even eat standing up! How did we get away from the traditional cradle of family unity, the kitchen table? I say it's high time we brought it back. Bringing back the function of the kitchen table will bring back our families' strength—which leads me to my next point.

We all know that building a family is all about teamwork. Sometimes we do things together, and sometimes we do things alone. But we must remember that whatever we do must benefit the family unit. It all works toward a common goal: to reflect who God is and to mirror Him. He wants us to be the light and the salt of the earth.

Think of God as a football coach and yourself as a player on His team. The players on the team are all different from each other. They think differently, look different, and have different personalities. Each family member has specific roles as well, but in order for a family to function as a team, we must operate and do what our coach tells us to do. He knows the rules of the game. He wants the team, the family, to win.

I know this isn't always easy. Many of us have atypical families. Gee, my own family is not typical. I have a fair share of crazy relatives and black sheep, but they all mean well. They are important to me. Whether I like it or not, I was born into my family, and they are who they are, and I am who I am. They each hold a special place in my heart. And they have had to be patient with me as well through the years. I went through a rebellious stage once upon a time. You see, I was very angry about the untimely death of my mother. My family members were very vocal in their disapproval of what I was doing with my life. Oh, how I simply wanted them to stay out of my business and leave me alone!

They bugged me to the moon and back again, but in retrospect, I realize that they did what they did because they cared. They never stopped loving me. I've gone through some really rocky times in my life, and my family has always been right there with me, through thick and thin—just like our Lord and Savior. Jesus leaves the past in the past, because He wants you to have a future with Him. Just as He loves us, we must love our families—no matter how much they make our blood boil at times. I'd like to share a tale with you about unconditional love.

A wife came into a minister's office one day, spitting nails, full of hatred for her husband. "I want to divorce him," she declared, "but before I do that, I want to hurt him as much as he has hurt me. I want to get even!"

The minister was taken aback, but keeping his composure, he suggested a plan. "Let's try something else," he said. "Go home and be your kindest to your husband. Praise him left and right. Go out of your way to be as kind, considerate, and generous as possible. Make him believe you still love him. After you've convinced him of your undying love and that you cannot live without him, drop the bomb. Tell him that you're getting a divorce. *That* will crush him." Satisfied, the woman smiled and exclaimed, "That is downright genius! Will he ever be surprised!"

The woman went home and put the plan into action immediately, really laying it on thick. For two months, she showed love and kindness—listening, giving, reinforcing, and sharing. The woman never returned to the minister's office, and he didn't hear from her by telephone, either. After some time, the minister called the woman and asked, "Are you ready to go through with the divorce?"

"Divorce?" she exclaimed. "No way! I discovered that I really *do* love him."

This story illustrates how unconditional love, lived out in daily life, will not only convince your family members that you love them, warts and all, but it will convince *you* that you love them! Unconditional love provides the nourishment your family needs to get through the things that Satan, the great home-wrecker, sends your way. In short, to hold grudges is to serve the Devil. Unconditional love—love with no strings attached—is the most important nourishment for your family. It lets every family member be "real," and that's a beautiful, marvelous thing!

Unconditional love may come naturally when it comes to loving your children. You might have to work on it some with your spouse. Try to remember your original vow to love and cherish in sickness and in health, for richer or poorer, for fat and skinny, in snoring and in fading beauty.

Have you ever heard the story of a man who fell for an opera singer? His only view of the singer was through binoculars from the third balcony. He basically fell in love with her voice. Oh, he just knew he could live happily ever after with a woman who had such a golden set of pipes! He barely noticed that she was considerably older than he was. Nor did he care that she walked with a limp. Surely her angelic voice would take them through life's roller coaster ride.

After a whirlwind courtship, they married. On the night of their honeymoon, the opera singer began to prepare for their first night together in their suite. As he watched in disbelief, she plucked out her glass eye and plopped it into a container on the nightstand. She pulled off her wig, ripped off her fake eyelashes, yanked out her dentures, unstrapped her artificial leg, and smiled at him as she slipped off her glasses that hid her hearing aid. Stunned and horrified, he gasped, "For goodness sake, woman, sing, sing, *sing*!"

For spouses, unconditional love begins with "I do," regardless of what is discovered later. As Jesus once told Peter in so many words, "You blew it, big-time. But it's okay because I'm going to use you, big-time." Jesus did not lose his temper with Peter. He did not "break up" with him. He forgave and ultimately restored him. The result of Christ's unconditional love *for* Peter was the return of unconditional love *from* Peter.

So, with this in mind, let us get back to the basics, back to square one: the Word of God. It is the "rule book" for families. Everything we need for a happy, well-adjusted family is in those pages. Just as there are instruction manuals for how to put together model airplanes, there are directions for God's children in the Bible. And just as we refer to the instructions to troubleshoot when a product is not working properly, we should go back to the basic directions in the Word of God. With this mind-set, let's bring back the glue that binds the family: the love that emanates from the kitchen table.

When our kids were small, we had family day on Thursdays. Each family member chose a theme for his or her night and planned what we would do and eat. Were those ever good times! I fondly remember "Italian Night" with lasagna, salad, garlic bread, and dessert. Sometimes after dinner was served, we would go bowling, watch a movie, or play board games. We did whatever the assigning family member chose, and we all participated.

As a grandmother, I continue that tradition. That day has changed to Tuesdays now, but the good times keep coming. I pick up my grandchildren, and we start our evenings by getting a light snack and doing homework. I prepare dinner, while my husband helps the grandchildren with their homework at—you guessed it—the kitchen table. Dinner is something of an event. Each child has jobs to prepare for dinner, including setting the table, pouring the drinks, etc. Once we sit down to dinner, the table talk starts off with informal conversation. Then we use this time for prayer, instruction, and encouragement.

After dinner, I allow the grandchildren to play games for about thirty minutes, letting them take turns choosing the games. No video games here! Their choices are games that stimulate their thinking, are fun, and keep the interaction going at the kitchen table. One of their favorites is a puzzle of the seven continents. I gave them that puzzle because it only consists of sixty pieces. Even after the puzzle is done, it's still a wonderful conversation piece for my grandbabies. We often talk at the table about the continents and what it's like to live in different places in the world.

Now it's your turn, dear reader. You may build on my routine or make one of your own. Remember, just as cars need fuel in order to function, our families needs fuel with the proper nourishment in order to function. As I stated earlier, unconditional love is the most crucial—and rare—ingredient that a family needs in order to be nourished.

Put aside any petty differences with family members. This is the time to let go of the resentment you felt about your teenage daughter borrowing your favorite sweater and losing it. Have a meeting and firmly lay down this new law: forgiving past grievances will be the first step to making the family closer and stronger. And that's what we are hoping to do here: to bring the family together, to get the family talking again, and to bring the family closer to Jesus.

So, no more eating in front of the television or alone in separate rooms and so on. Here are the kitchen-table rules. Once everyone is seated:

- No cell phones are allowed. This is the most important rule, especially for teenagers. What's the point of sitting with people when you are texting or talking on the phone?
- Take turns. Everyone eats, so why shouldn't everyone talk? Don't interrupt.
- Share high and lows. The lows are not fun, but they are important. This opens up the floor to encouragement or good advice.
- Pray and take prayer requests. The father usually prays first and sets the example. Then the father calls on other family members to pray. We are teaching the children that there is an order that God has set for the family, and it is an incredible bonding tool. Just as the popular saying goes, a family that prays together stays together.

- Communicate. Discuss family values. In our home, family values are rules or ideals that, as a family, we have agreed to live by and stay true to. Having well-defined family values helps solidify the foundation for a strong family. When cultivated long enough, this closeness provides a soft place to fall when life doesn't go according to plan. Strong and consistent family values are important in building trust and confidence in each family member. We communicate these values at our kitchen table.

Let me suggest ten values that I live by, which you might consider for your own family.

1. Belonging

It is important that all members of my family feel that they are loved, that they belong, and that they matter. Being a cohesive family could mean that you spend every spare minute together doing family activities, but keep in mind that everyone is different. Creating a strong family unit is great, but each person should be allowed the space and freedom to explore the activities they think they might enjoy. People are more courageous and more willing to take chances if they know they have a safe place to come back to when things don't quite work out. Coming together for special occasions and holidays and just spending time together as a family are what help build that sense of belonging.

2. Flexibility

I'm all for order, schedules, and structure in my family to help maintain some level of sanity. But too much structure—and unwillingness to give a little—can result in a lot of unhappiness and resentment. The more flexibility you allow in decision-making, for example, the happier your family will be for it. Imagine what it would be like if one member of the family always thought he was right and enforced his way of doing things. This certainly wouldn't lead to much happiness within the family unit.

3. Respect

This is a bit more difficult to define. For my family, respecting each other means taking into account others' feelings, thoughts, needs, and preferences when making decisions. It also means acknowledging and valuing everyone's thoughts, feelings, and contributions to the family as a whole.

Respect is indeed earned, and there is a very fine line between it and fear. The only way to earn and keep someone's respect is to first show them respect yourself. Respect, as an important family value, will extend outside the home and into school, work, or other social settings.

4. Honesty

This is the foundation of all relationships that are meant to last: mother–daughter, husband–wife, sister–brother, and so on. Without honesty, a deeper connection will not form and certainly won't last. We should encourage honesty by practicing understanding and respect when someone tells us of their wrongdoings. If we lose it and get angry when we're told what has happened, the other person will be more likely to hide the problem from us the next time, simply to avoid the disrespect.

5. Forgiveness

Forgiving people who have wronged us is an important choice to make. Yes, forgiveness is a choice. It is not some feeling that randomly washes over us when we feel the other person has "suffered" enough. This can be tough, since a lot of us tend to equate forgiveness with approval of the action. They are *not* the same thing. Holding a grudge is not conducive to a close family with mutual respect.

Keep in mind that everyone makes mistakes, we all occasionally say things we wish we hadn't, and none of us are perfect. Refer to Value #8 on communication. Get issues out in the open, gain some understanding, and move on. Life is too short to waste on grudges.

6. Generosity

Giving without thinking about "what's in it for me" is an important value for anyone wanting to be a responsible, contributing member to society. Generosity builds empathy, because it causes us to think more about what people want or need. Being generous doesn't mean simply handing over money to someone in need. It can also include giving your time, love, attention, or even some of your possessions.

7. Curiosity

Children have a natural curiosity. If you've ever watched a toddler, even for a couple of minutes, you've seen that quality shine through. For some people, that curiosity wanes. I think it's important to encourage and push our kids, and even ourselves, to be curious about things. Rarely should we just take someone's word for something. How do we spark our curiosity? By asking questions. Lots of them. Read about a topic you know very little about, and don't be afraid to say you don't know something. Critical thinking is an important skill that can be learned and developed by exploring your own curiosity.

8. Communication

Communication is as much an art as it is a science. Failure to communicate will likely lead to unhappiness and misunderstanding. Small issues grow into larger ones, and when they eventually boil to the surface, it's unlikely they will be resolved calmly. Communication is a lot more than simply speaking your mind. In addition to spoken words, communication also extends to tone, volume, expression, eye contact, body language, and effective listening.

I would argue that this is the most important value for families to have. When people feel they can talk openly about anything—hopes, dreams, fears, successes, or failures—all without judgment, they are encouraged and their bonds are strengthened.

9. Responsibility

We'd all like to be considered responsible people. Some of us are, and some of us are decidedly less so. Responsibility is something that is learned. As a child, you might have been shown how to put your toys away after playing, how to tidy your room, or how and when to feed the dog. This sense of responsibility extends well into adulthood. An adult who has an intrinsic sense of responsibility doesn't require a lot of prodding to show up to work on time, return phone calls, or meet deadlines. Setting out individual responsibilities for family members works to instill this quality in everyone.

10. Traditions

This is by far the most fun for me. I think traditions are what make a family unique; they draw people together and create a sense of belonging for everyone. Traditions don't need to be expensive, elaborate, or burdensome. A tradition can be something as simple as a lazy Saturday morning, sipping coffee and chatting, or an annual pot of black-eye peas to ring in the New Year. If you don't currently have traditions in your family, create them! All traditions start with one person. Why not let *your* family start a tradition?

Remember when I said that the family is a team? As we all know, teams have action plans. This schedule may be of assistance. Customize it to your liking.

Daily Chores

- Makes beds.
- Wash dishes.
- Check bathroom.
- Pick up rooms.
- Pick up kitchen.

Weekly Chores

- Monday: plan your menu, change beds
- Tuesday: wash, vacuum
- Wednesday: iron, mop floors
- Thursday: dust, grocery-shop, take and pick up laundry
- Friday: clean bathroom, enjoy a free afternoon and lunch date with a friend
- Saturday: do yard work, clean the car inside and out
- Sunday: rest and go to church with your family

Monthly Chores

- Week 1: clean stove
- Week 2: clean refrigerator
- Week 3: clean washer and dryer
- Week 4: sweep and organize garage

A kitchen consists of several amenities in the home. Please keep all your appliances clean, your pantry organized, and your cabinets, countertops, and sink clean. Don't forget that your floors need to be mopped and waxed. Once your kitchen is clean and organized, maintain it!

Yes, a happy family in Christ takes work, but it's a labor of love well worth the effort. May you build many fond memories at your kitchen table, dear reader. Amen.

My Homework Assignment for Chapter 4

1.

2.

3.

4.

5.

6.

Chapter 5

Bathroom: A Scent of Self-Worth

The way you treat yourself sets the standard for others.
—Dr. Sonya Friedman

Don't ask yourself what the world needs; ask yourself
what makes you come alive. And then go and do that.
Because what the world needs are
people who have come alive.
—Howard Washington Thurman

Godly women, let's walk into one of my favorite rooms: the bathroom. It's the place in the home that we visit first thing in the morning and the last place we visit before turning in. No matter what time we enter that room, we emerge from it refreshed and reenergized.

Opal once asked me, "Hattie, what fragrance do you use in your bathroom? It really does smell good. Your bathroom is decorated very nicely too. It's so clean, and it smells really good. I know I keep saying that, but it does."

"Thank you!" I replied.

"How did you learn how to decorate your home so well? You must have a gift of decorating," Opal pursued.

I do. I am so grateful that God gave me that gift. Women are all gifted—but in different areas. However, this is a small area where you can acquire a flair. In no time, you can have your bathroom decorated, organized, and clean.

Our Christ-centered home is a haven of rest—in every room. When my spouse comes in from work, the first place he goes is the bathroom. I do my best to keep it neat, clean, and smelling good for him.

Have you ever needed to use a bathroom, only to be sorely disappointed when you got there because it was dingy, dirty, and smelled unpleasant? We all have had this experience—whether it's in our own homes, at a friend's house, or in a public place. And how did you feel? It's safe to say you left feeling disgusted and unclean yourself. It was probably a truly unpleasant memory if the place was a restaurant. How did you feel about eating there afterward?

Your bathroom is one of the most used rooms in your house. Don't spend your time in an ugly, messy, mismatched bathroom! Your bathroom is also a reflection of you. When you start seeing yourself the way God sees you, it reflects in your actions. Your effort and imagination can turn this room into the attractive space you want it to be. Decorating your bathroom is fun and exciting, and it lets your family, friends, and guests know just how much you value them and appreciate them, just as I honor my hardworking husband this way.

First of all, is your sense of *self* well-decorated? If we have developed good self-esteem, we will look at our bathrooms differently. I, like many women, have often been confused by the differences between what I hear on TV, what my mother tells me, and what my girlfriends say. But I have realized that none of those comments define me. Our self-esteem is not based on what we hear on talk shows or on what our mothers, girlfriends, or coworkers say. It is only what God thinks of you that matters. Please sit down, and let's discover and define what self-esteem is.

When I was growing up, I had many hang-ups, and I really didn't like myself. I was tall and skinny and had so much hair that my father constantly thinned it out because it was so bushy. Oh, how I envied my sisters' lighter complexions. Even though I received lots of compliments, I didn't feel good about myself. People told me all the time that I was outgoing, smart, had a great personality, was creative, had great faith, and dressed fashionably.

But I didn't appreciate myself until later on in my life when I was in Guam and went to a women's Bible study. They talked about identity. I learned that, as women, we foolishly base our worth on our looks, our feelings, guilt about our pasts, and the way others view us. I saw what a waste of time this was. Thank God, these older women taught me God's Word and His principles, and they were models for me to live by. For the first time, I was set free from the lies of the Devil.

The technical definition of *self-esteem* is "feelings of worth based on skills, accomplishments, status, financial resources, or appearance ..." Blah, blah, blah. This definition of *self-esteem* implies that people should indulge in prideful self-worship, casting God aside.

James 4:6 tells us that "God is opposed to the proud, but gives grace to the humble."

If we only adore our worldly possessions, we are left with foolish pride. Jesus told us, "When you do all the things which are commanded you, say, "We are unworthy slaves; we have done only that which we ought to have done" (Luke 17:10).

This does not mean that Christians should have low self-esteem. Please reject the stereotype the world paints of God-loving people as simple-minded, boring, plain, unimportant, and worthless. Self-worth is not defined by our occupations or accomplishments, even if we are working for God. When we lay down our pride before Him, He will honor us.

Psalm 16:2 reminds us, "You are my Lord! I have no good besides You."

The most effective action for building self-esteem in Christians is a right relationship with God. We know our value because of the high price God paid for us through the blood of His Son, Jesus Christ. When we have healthy self-esteem, we value ourselves enough to not become enslaved by the demons of: greed, jealousy, arrogance, stinginess, and so forth. Instead, we should conduct ourselves with humility and treat others with the same compassion we want for ourselves.

"Do nothing from selfishness or empty conceit, but with humility of mind regard one another as more important than yourselves" (Philippians 2:3). "For through the grace given to me I say to everyone among you not to think more highly of himself than he ought to think; but to think so as to have sound judgment, as God has allotted to each a measure of faith" (Romans 12:3).

Be honest in your estimate of yourself, measuring your value by how much faith God has given you. If you haven't done this fully yet, accept your new identity in Christ:

"I have been crucified with Christ; and it is no longer I who live, but Christ lives in me; and the life which I now live in the flesh I live by faith in the Son of God, who loved me and gave Himself up for me" (Galatians 2:20).

Now you know who you are. You are totally forgiven, fully accepted and loved by your heavenly Father. When we know this, nothing matters except what God's Word declares for our lives. Then we can truly identify with Christ alone.

So, we are ready for a new bathroom for the new you!

First of all, consider the mood you want to incorporate into this room using scent. Smells are among the most powerful forces in the human experience. They can instantly change one of life's best moments into one of life's worst moments. Or they have the ability to do the opposite: to change one of life's worst moments into one of life's cherished moments. How many times has a certain smell taken you back years, or even decades, to a particular memory? We are looking for that same kind of association here.

> But thanks be to God, who always leads
> us in His triumph in Christ, and manifests
> through us the sweet aroma of the knowledge

of Him in every place. For we are a fragrance of Christ to God among those who are being saved and among those who are perishing; to the one an aroma from death to death, to the other an aroma from life to life. And who is adequate for these things? For we are not like many, peddling the word of God; but as from sincerity, but as from God, we speak in Christ in the sight of God. (2 Corinthians 2:14–17)

The fragrance of a godly woman is the scent of faith. Proverbs 31:10–31(MSG) tells us:

> A good woman is hard to find, and worth far more than diamonds.
>
> Her husband trusts her without reserve, and never has reason to regret it.
>
> Never spiteful, she treats him generously all her life long.
>
> She shops around for the best yarns and cottons, and enjoys knitting and sewing.
>
> She's like a trading ship that sails to faraway places and brings back exotic surprises.
>
> She's up before dawn, preparing breakfast for her family and organizing her day.
>
> She looks over a field and buys it, then, with money she's put aside, plants a garden.

First thing in the morning, she dresses for
work, rolls up her sleeves, eager to get
started.

She senses the worth of her work, is in no
hurry to call it quits for the day.

She's skilled in the crafts of home and hearth,
diligent in homemaking.

She's quick to assist anyone in need, reaches
out to help the poor.

She doesn't worry about her family when it
snows; their winter clothes are all mended
and ready to wear.

She makes her own clothing, and dresses in
colorful linens and silks.

Her husband is greatly respected when he
deliberates with the city fathers.

She designs gowns and sells them, brings the
sweaters she knits to the dress shops.

Her clothes are well-made and elegant, and
she always faces tomorrow with a smile.

When she speaks she has something
worthwhile to say, and she always says it
kindly.

She keeps an eye on everyone in her household,
and keeps them all busy and productive.

Her children respect and bless her; her husband
joins in with words of praise:

"Many women have done wonderful things,
  but you've outclassed them all!"
Charm can mislead and beauty soon fades.
The woman to be admired and praised is the
  woman who lives in the Fear-of-GOD.
Give her everything she deserves!
Festoon her life with praises!

You can plainly see that before the foundation of the world, God designed women to be the fragrance of salvation, the fragrance of submission in our homes, the fragrance of respect to our husbands, and the fragrance of a priceless woman.

Let's take a moment to talk about the fragrance of respect. "Show respect for everyone. Love your Christian brothers and sisters. Fear God. Show respect for the king" (1 Peter 2:17).

God clearly tells us to respect everyone. We are not to base our respect on what a person does or does not do. We are not to base our respect on relationships. To be obedient to God means to respect our husbands, children, coworkers, and even the homeless man on the street. By showing respect, we are also showing love; they are almost one and the same.

Does showing respect mean that I agree with everything a person says or does? No, it does not. Showing respect is not based on agreement. The Bible is clear that every person is to be in subjection to the governing authorities.

"For there is no authority except from God, and those which exist are established by God" (Romans 13:1). This can be applied to modern-day situations, as there are individuals in positions of authority right now that we may not agree with. However, God has allowed them to be placed in their positions, and we must respect them. There are people in our families that we did not choose to be related to, but that does not take away our responsibility to show them respect.

The best way to know whether or not you are showing respect to another is to ask how you would want to be treated. Many of us have individuals in our lives who are struggling with various issues: financial difficulties, divorces, relationship breakups, weight problems, and emotional distress behind relationships. It's more difficult to be respected when people have warned us that we were headed for trouble and we didn't listen.

Whatever the issue a person is dealing with, whether it is self-imposed or not, we are still expected to show him or her respect.

Do you have any relationships where you have begun to disrespect someone because of your opinions? Do you see a friend struggling financially, but you are unconcerned and will not even pray for them because you think they got into it because of their poor decisions and spending habits? Do you have a friend who is overweight, but you have no compassion because you see their eating habits and you think: why bother?

Challenge yourself through the Holy Spirit's leadership to identify the relationships where you have begun to show disrespect, and ask God to show you how to move back into a loving, respectful relationship. What are some signs of disrespect? There are many, but here are some of the most prominent.

- Disregard for other people's feelings
- Not listening or allowing them to share their opinions or feelings
- Cutting people off when they are talking
- Talking over other people
- Talking to people while walking away from them
- Being rude or insensitive
- Rolling your eyes or doing some other action that shows an unloving attitude
- Using profanity in your conversation with them
- Talking down to other people
- Making fun of what other people are saying

Do any of these describe your behavior in relationships? If they do, I encourage you to pray and ask God to show you how to renew your respect in these relationships and how to honor and respect those that you are in relationship with.

" In everything, therefore, treat people the same way you want them to treat you, for this is the Law of the Prophet" (Matthew 7:12).

All these fragrances—faith, salvation, and respect—are eternal and have been purchased for us through Jesus Christ our Lord. They are free of charge and have the smell of life, not death.

Anyway, back to the bathroom. When we enter a bathroom, the first thing we notice—besides the smell—is the cleanliness and order. This usually determines whether or not we want to use it. When your bathroom is fresh-smelling and neat, it becomes inviting. It beckons everyone, saying, "Come in and use me. Stay for a while." Isn't this the purpose of a bathroom, to be a place of relief, refuge, and renewal? Think "mini spa." Give this room some TLC. Here is a checklist:

- Clean the toilet. Scrub inside the bowl, and wipe down the seat with disinfectant.
- Clean the sink. Scrub with scouring powder.
- Clean the tub. This is most important. Why wash up in a dirty tub? You might as well jump in the mud! There are many products on the market for keeping soap scum at bay. Use them!
- Clean the mirror. Enhance that reflection of you. Keep it sparkling and free of toothpaste splatters.
- Organize everything. Make sure everything is in its place. This is an especially daunting task for ladies with our hair products, styling aids, and cosmetics. Make use of the sink drawers. Invest in baskets, and keep hair-care items under the sink cabinets.

- Mop the floor. If you have tile floors in your bathroom, they need freshening up now and then.
- Wash rugs. These rugs get as much traffic as your living room rugs. Throw them in the machine at least once a month.

Cleaning the bathrooms in your home can seem like a chore. But the good news is that the tedious part is over. The fun is in the decorating, making it plush and comforting as you surround yourself with things you love. Here are a couple tips to transform your bathroom into a place that is inviting and attractive.

Aromatherapy

We talked earlier about how important fragrance is in influencing moods, so choose scents that you enjoy or scents the whole family enjoys. Let's recognize the many wonderful scents God has bestowed upon us and celebrate them in our bathrooms. You can experiment with everything from fruits to floral scents, ocean breezes to musky vanilla. You can burn incense for a few minutes. Lighting a good-quality, scented candle is a great way to uplift your morning too. Look for non-toxic air fresheners. Use scented oils that you can heat up in a mini Crock-Pot or with a candle. Keep scented potpourri or scented satchels throughout the bathroom. There are aromatherapy products available at all price points. For the greatest savings, choose products that are inexpensive to maintain. For example, incense, scented oils, and candles can be found at discount stores.

Personality and Style

Place attractive and serene images on your bathroom walls. Think of the bathroom as your private spa. Snapshots of memorable vacation spots can be blown up and framed. Browse the home-goods section of discount stores. They are a gold mine for small yet pretty pictures for this room. These places also carry beautiful fabric shower curtains, rugs, and bathroom furniture. Add a full-length mirror to at least one wall of the bathroom for extra pizzazz.

Keeping the bathroom clean is easier when it is a desirable room. Family members who once avoided the bathroom may actually try to spend a few extra moments there, once you make it over. Encourage all of your family members to get in on the act of maintaining the bathroom. It is now your spa within the home!

My Homework Assignment for Chapter 5

1.

2.

3.

4.

5.

6.

Chapter 6

Bedroom: Relationships

Some of the biggest challenges in relationships come
from the fact that most people enter a relationship in
order to get something: they're trying to find someone
who's going to make them feel good. In reality, the only
way a relationship will last is if you see your relationship
as a place that you go to give and not a
place that you go to take.
—Anthony Robbins

The glue that holds all relationships together, including
the relationship between the leader and the led, is trust,
and trust is based on integrity.
—Brian Tracy

W e've talked a great deal about relationships and how much they matter in the pursuit of a godly home. How's it going so far? You can measure your progress by answering the following questions:

- Are you honoring Jesus as the head of the family?
- Do you know Jesus as your Savior and Lord?
- Are you submitting to and cooperating with the members of God's family in your life?
- Are you showing respect and support to your husband?
- Are you submitting to your husband out of reverence and respect for Christ?

At this point, I hope you answer yes! Now, let's take a walk to our final room—the bedroom. This room reflects how you view your relationship with your spouse. Don't feel left out if you are not married. Singles, this pertains to you too. I speak to all women—married and single—with this statement: have patience and learn all you can about the Word of God. Let's not get tired of doing the right thing; for at the right time, you will reap a magnificent harvest.

"The Lord is not slow about His promise, as some count slowness, but is patient toward you, not wishing for any to perish but for all to come to repentance" (2 Peter 3:9).

If I asked you what your most important relationship was, what would you tell me? Is it your relationship with your husband or wife, your parents, or your children? Would you say it was a coworker or a good friend? If someone who did not know you very well looked at your life, what would he or she identify as your most important relationship based on the way you treat it?

Most of us will say that our relationship with God is the most important. We might claim that, but is it true? Would someone on the outside be able to tell by the way we talk, walk, or act, or would they be totally shocked by our answer? Truthfully, people ought to be able to tell who we are in relationships with. They should be able to determine the strength of the relationship based on how we act and what we say.

What are some of the signs of a true-love relationship, whether it is a relationship with our Creator or a relationship with another human being?

- We spend our time on the relationship, which indicates where our hearts are.

- We spend our money on the relationship, which shows what we treasure.
- We want to learn more about this person, and we do things we know will make him happy and put a smile on his face.
- We exhibit selflessness, not selfishness.
- We give sacrificially.
- We give up the desire or need to be right, because the relationship is more important than being right.

Are these things any different if our love relationship is with God rather than another human being? They should not be. Our mates may claim to know us inside and out, but God knows us on a much deeper level. He knows our end from our beginning.

"For God so loved the world, that he gave his only begotten Son, that whosoever believeth in him should not perish, but have everlasting life" (John 3:16 KJV).

That, my dear reader, is true love! Have you ever had a relationship with that kind of pure, selfless love? God's love is a free gift. It has no strings attached. When you love someone, you do things for him or her without hesitation. You just want to give that person happiness.

God is patiently waiting for us to love Him back, to love Him enough to forsake the sin that so easily besets us, to love Him so much that we put Him first and show it—by *doing* rather than just *talking* about it. How much time do you spend with God on a daily basis? Remember that God is a jealous God. Exodus 34:14 says, "For you shall not worship any other god, for the Lord, whose name is Jealous, is a jealous God." He is not into sharing. God will go to war with and for you. Nobody loves you more.

So instead of chasing after all that glitters and satisfies temporarily, chase God and allow Him to work out life's details. Chase Him by studying the Word, spending time with Him in prayer and meditation, worship and praise. If you spend the time with Him first and make Him a priority, He will teach you how to make your other relationships right. He will improve things that you didn't even know needed a makeover, revealing the error and guiding you in the right direction to save and preserve life—yours as well as the lives of others connected to you.

If you have not yet realized what your most important relationship should be, I will tell you that it's not your husband, son or daughter, mother or father. Your most important relationship is the one you have with God through His Son, Jesus Christ. Allow it to direct and be the foundation of the relationships you have with everyone else.

Take some time to evaluate the present condition of your relationship with God. How does it look? Don't fool yourself into thinking that you can have a bad relationship with others and still have a great relationship with Him. It does not work that way! Our relationships with others are a direct manifestation of our relationship with God. If you are ignoring the people who have shown you the most love, if you are disregarding them or their feelings, know that this not the Holy Spirit's way.

I shared with you before that God has improved my relationships with the people in my life—at work, in ministry, and in my personal life. I thought I was okay, but He showed me that I was not. There were some things He wanted to correct, and that's just what He has done. He showed me a spirit of rebellion in one of my relationships. That inability to submit was disobedience to Him and worked against what He had told me to do.

It's your turn. This is the time to make any necessary course corrections and put the focus on God. Allow Him to work in you and your relationships, starting with your relationship with Him. It is time to bring God's love into your bedroom.

Our bedrooms are our private peace chambers. We rise from this room with rejuvenation and wonder to face each new day that the Lord hath made. When we are small, the bedroom is a toy wonderland and a place for unlimited imagination. When we are adults, the bedroom is a place of relaxation and refuge. No matter what our age, this room is like a best friend that "just gets us." It's a best friend that we have a history with. Our bedrooms have seen many tears and much laughter, and we all want to give our best care to our best friend, don't we? So here we go.

Color me peaceful.

Just as I talked about scent influencing our moods in the bathroom, colors have that same potential. Reds and pinks scream, while neutrals are quiet. Blues and greens soothe, and yellow invigorates. God gave us so many beautiful, vibrant hues! What aura do you wish to bring into your boudoir? Whatever color scheme you choose, try to establish balance. If you go with a predominantly neutral palette, accent it with bright colors. If you have a bright color scheme, keep your walls fairly "vanilla," and scale back on the accessories. Feel free to incorporate scents here like you do with the bathroom. There are varieties of plug-ins, potpourri, and incense. Whatever you do, have fun with this!

Call to order.

An orderly master bedroom is conducive to what matters most: love for God and love for your mate. It reflects a wife's love and devotion to her spouse. Inversely, an unkempt bedroom suggests indifference toward the relationship. Make a concerted effort to keep only furniture that gets used. The closet can be a nightmare or a dream, depending upon how well you maintain it. Donate all clothes and shoes that you have not worn in six months to a year; resolve to get rid of something when you bring new things into the closet. Are you still storing a shoebox in there that's bulging with receipts and old check carbons? Why? Get it out of there! Invest in a hamper instead of chucking dirty clothes on the floor. When your surroundings are clutter-free, so is your mind. Then you have the undivided attention to give to the Lord and your mate.

Lay down rules.

You and your mate should ensure that your place of peace and refuge is protected. Establish rules that keep the bedroom enveloped in serenity and order. This can involve anything from prohibiting food in the bedroom to leaving arguments outside the bedroom door. This is an opportunity for you and your mate to come together as a team with God's help.

To keep the Holy Spirit in your bedroom and in your relationship, remember this: "God created man in his own image, in the image of God He created him; males and females He created them" (Genesis 1:27).

All relationships should reflect these five things:

1. You been created to fellowship with God as Adam talked with God.
2. You have been created to represent God in the earth. God created the earth, set it in order, and then turned it over to man. So you and I are here as God's representatives.
3. You have been created to fulfill God-given assignments. God told Adam to name all the creatures, which he did. God told Adam to take

care of the garden, which he did. So like Adam, we are here to fulfill God-given assignments.

4. You've been created to express God's lordship. When Adam and Eve obeyed God daily, it was an expression of God's lordship over their lives.

5. We were created to leave a godly, righteous deposit in the earth.

And know this:

* Marriage is a gift.
* Marriage is an opportunity to learn how to love.
* Marriage is built upon a commitment to communicate. We have to learn how to speak our partner's language.

I really stress this last point: communication. Silence is not always golden. Some people take the principle of not talking too much to the extreme and hardly say anything at all. In fact, they feel justified in using the silent treatment. There are numerous reasons for this response. Some use silence as a means to avoid controversy or as a weapon to control, frustrate, or manipulate. Sometimes a husband or a wife takes the pathway of silence because it seems to be the least painful; perhaps one spouse is not a ready listener, or a spouse has been hurt so deeply that it keeps him silent. I encourage you to start talking. So many conflicts could be avoided with open lines of communication.

I talked about the role of a wife earlier, and I'd like to review it, as it is critical in creating a godly home. "Wives, be subject to your own husbands, as to the Lord. For the husband is the head of the wife, as Christ also is the head of the church, He Himself being the Savior of the body. But as the church is subject to Christ, so also the wives ought to be to their husbands in everything" (Ephesians 5:22–24).

I know what you are thinking. Please don't take the above Scripture literally. At the time Ephesians was written, husbands were the lords over their wives, and wives were more or less like property, not having an opinion on the way things were to be done. Their purpose was to serve their man, like a master–slave relationship instead of partners. Paul presented a rather revolutionary idea in that a husband and wife were *equals* in Christ, submitting to each other. It's interesting that he didn't spend much time telling women to be submissive to their husbands, because the culture of that time had already trained them well in that respect. He just reminded them that when they were wholly committed to serving the Lord, they would submit to their husbands as a natural expression of their commitment to Christ.

Our culture is vastly different now. Because of "women's lib," there is a demand for equality between men and women in the workplace and in the home. Popular sitcoms often depict the woman as superior and the man as incompetent. The acceptance of divorce as an answer to tough relationships has skewed the picture of marriage away from the way God intended it to be. Oftentimes, the children become the focus of the family rather than the husband-and-wife relationship. How can we, as women who love and serve God, show submission to our husbands without being accused of being doormats?

The answer, dear reader, is found in Ephesians 5:22–24, mentioned above. Keeping in mind that both partners are equal in God's eyes, marriage is like being on a team. Along with a coach, every team has a captain. That captain calls the plays, puts people in the positions where they function best, and expects everyone to work together. He has the responsibility to know the people on his team well enough to use their abilities and gifts in a way that enhances the team's ability to win.

When the team responds to his leadership and works together, not much can stand in their way. However, when team members all do their own thing, there is division, and the team doesn't do well. Sometimes the captain will put someone else in the dominant position because he knows that will benefit the team more. But the captain always remains the captain, being responsible to lead the team in the best direction.

In marrying our husbands, we made a decision to accept him as the leader (under God) of our relationship. It's to our benefit to understand the man we married and support him. Marriage involves working together yet allowing your husband to be the main man. Each person gives to the relationship what is needed to have a winning team. Sometimes you will play a major role in a certain area, while he is doing something else equally important. So how do we play, live, and fulfill our positions on the team?

Understand who your husband is. God has gifted each man with a unique style of leadership. Some take charge and lead the way, getting things done in an efficient manner. Some are more visionary, following a dream. Others are steady, sometimes slow to make a decision but always ready to help others. Be ready to support your husband in whatever way will make him a successful leader in your relationship and home.

Let your husband take the lead. No matter what the personality of your husband may be, let him be the leader. Allow him the freedom to make decisions without pressure. He has the final say on decisions that affect everyone. Respect his decisions: no grumbling. You are a team! Most major decisions are made after discussions between husband and wife. Once you have both prayed, you will receive the truth. The truth is God's view of the matter and your husband's final decision. It will most likely reflect a combination of both of your opinions. Sometimes decisions are impulsive; let the consequences be what they are. Don't berate him for what you might consider a foolish decision. He will figure it out after a while without your help.

I'm sure you are wondering why respect so important to a man. A woman once wrote, in so many words, that disrespect to men is equivalent to being despised. She also said that respecting your husband significantly contributes to his happiness in your relationship. It's difficult for him to feel loved without your respect. A man once stated, "When my wife admires me, I'll do anything for her." A man may look like a lion on the outside, but show him a little respect and he becomes a loving lamb. Are you with me, godly sisters?

The dictionary defines *respect* this way: "to feel or show honor or esteem for; hold in high regard; courteous expressions of regard." *Honor* means: "to respect greatly; regard highly; esteem; to show great respect or high regard for; treat with deference and courtesy." *Admiration* is "the act of admiring; the sense of wonder, delight, and pleased approval inspired by anything fine, skillful, beautiful, etc."

As you can imagine, the opposite of respect, honor, and admiration are disrespect, contempt, and disdain. Here's how to tell if you are dabbling in these relationship-killers:

1. Do I contradict or question my husband in front of others, or do I discuss my questions with him in private?
2. Do I openly criticize him or openly praise him (or don't rub it in when he is wrong)?
3. Do I belittle his efforts to show affection, help out, or respond with affection and appreciation?
4. Do I complain, or do I display a positive attitude toward my husband?
5. Do I constantly remind him of unfinished tasks and take his matters into my hands, or do I give

a gentle reminder and then trust him to do his tasks?

6. Do I act as his conscience, or do I pray for the Holy Spirit to work in him?

7. Do I compare my husband negatively with others, or do I express genuine admiration?

8. Do I respond with rudeness or sarcasm, or do I show respect with tone, facial expressions, and body language?

9. Do I withhold information, or do I act honestly?

10. Do I ignore my husband's needs and desires, or do I make his needs and desires my priority?

To make a long story short, we expect our husbands to love us even on our bad days, so we must do the same for them.

"Nevertheless, each individual among you also is to love his own wife even as himself, and the wife must see to it that she respects her husband" (Ephesians 5:25, 33).

To summarize the importance of our submission to our husbands, consider the following from *The Life Application Study Bible*: "God ordained submission in certain relationships to prevent chaos. It is essential to understand that submission is not surrender, withdrawal, or apathy."

This does not indicate inferiority, because God created all people in His image, and all have equal value. Submission is willingly putting oneself under the authority of another.

Our submission to our husbands does not happen because we are weaker. It happens because we are strong enough to understand that a team needs a leader and that God has called the husband to be that person.

Wives, understand and support your husbands in ways that show your support for Christ. The husband provides leadership to his wife the way Christ does to his church, not by domineering but by cherishing. Just as the church submits to Christ as He exercises such leadership, wives should likewise submit to their husbands. (Angela Willingham, CEO of New Beginnings Holistic Fitness Ministries, INC. What Is Your Most Important Relationship? January 30, 2012 Website www.mynewtemple.org)

For Single Ladies

I want to put a positive spin on singleness. When you are single, you have time to devote your allegiance to the Lord and to the work of God without distraction. A great example of this is found in the widowed single woman, Ruth, the Moabite who left her country and people to go with her mother-in-law, Naomi, to Bethlehem. She did not pursue a husband; rather she pursued a calling to serve Naomi, desiring that the God of Israel become her God (Ruth 1:15–18). However, in the course of pursuing that calling, God brought her to the attention of a man named Boaz, who was blessed by Ruth's heart of servitude and who pursued her for marriage (Ruth 2–4).

Singles, you are so special to God, and He loves you so much! I know you might be in a state that you do not desire.

Just know that there is a time for all things. You may be a woman who has never been married or a woman who is divorced. You may be a widowed woman who has suffered the loss of your spouse, or a young lady who is too young to be married. Or perhaps you are single by choice. Whatever the case, God has you in a holding pattern, preparing you to answer your calling.

When you do answer your calling, learn how to operate in it. Put God first in everything you do, and receive his viewpoint on all matters. Learn how to be a good servant, and be content with the season where you are. Seasons will change and your situation will too. Learn how to honor God in every room of your home, and when God sends you your Boaz, you will know what to do to please your man. As you please him, you are pleasing God, for the Bible says, "He who finds a wife finds a good thing and obtains favor from the LORD" (Proverbs 18:22).

You are a good thing, because everything that God created was good. "God saw all that He had made, and behold, it was very good. And there was evening and there was morning, the sixth day" (Genesis 1:31). God knows where you are, and He knows how to cause the right man's path to meet yours. "For everything created by God is good, and nothing is to be rejected if it is received with gratitude" (1 Timothy 4:4).

I speak from experience on this matter. When I was single, I lived in California, worked for a car insurance company, and went to church every time the door was open.

I loved church, and my apartment was a block from it. I was in my early twenties, single, and desiring to meet my husband. I prayed that God would send me one. I had been hurt badly in a relationship, and I had declared that I would wait on the Lord and that He would give me the desires of my heart. Oh, how I wanted to be married! But I didn't date anyone for years.

At this point in my life, I visited my sister while on vacation in Colorado. She set me up on a blind date with a man who would later become my husband. I fell in love with him right away. I asked him what he thought about marriage. He said he didn't want to marry until he was in his thirties, and he was twenty-six at the time. Boo hoo! But I trusted in the Lord and waited patiently. It paid off, and later we married!

To make a long story short: singles, when you are faithful to God, He is faithful to you. If it's a mate you desire, let Him handle it. He knows just what to do.

In the meantime, there are so many people who need your love besides a man. There are shelters, mentoring programs for children, and other special-interest clubs. Spread God's love around, and He will eventually bring it back to you tenfold.

Whether you have a ring on your finger or not, it's important to keep God first. We are to trust Him completely. Having God in your heart and in your home just naturally attracts the right kind of love.

Spiritual Points

1. *Keep making time for each other.* This isn't always easy, especially if you both have demanding and hectic careers, a family, pets, or other responsibilities. It isn't always easy, but it is important. When things are good, we may not feel the need to set time aside specifically to work on our relationship or to connect with each other; we already feel pretty good and pretty connected. We take each other for granted. But slowly, over time, the distance can grow, and before long the *need* is there to feel connected again.

2. *Improve the way you talk to each other.* Communication is a vital part of any relationship. Some couples can get in a rut of disrespect and insults. Initially, it may be funny and a bit of an inside joke, but it can get old and become disrespectful and abrasive. Take a look at how you speak to the people who matter the most to you. Would say the same thing to your colleagues or in the presence of your neighbors? If not, consider cleaning up your act a bit. Speak to each other with respect and kindness; make this a habit.

3. *Make an effort.* When I was a stay-at-home mom, I came to realize how easy it was to choose comfort over style when it came to getting dressed in the morning. For an extended period of time, old pants and my husband's sweatshirts were my daily attire. But I got tired of feeling frumpy and not looking my best.

Making an effort when it comes to your appearance shows respect for yourself and for your partner. Now, I'm not saying you need to have black-tie dinners each night or scrub toilets in heels and your Sunday best. What I'm saying is to take a bit of pride in how you present yourself: brush your hair, put on a bit of makeup, change out of work clothes for dinner—simple things. It does wonders for you self-esteem, and it shows that you're making an effort for your own sake as well as for your partner.

4. *Don't keep score.* Keeping score is one of the most damaging things you can do to your relationship. I did the dishes last night, I took the garbage out last week; it's his turn to do the laundry; it's her turn to clean the bathroom. Keeping score leads to resentment, hard feelings, and a whole lot of stuff not getting done around the house. If you find yourself starting to keep score, *stop*! Get together and talk about joint responsibilities. Set realistic expectations. Talk openly about feeling as if you're being taken for granted. Suggest ways the other person can pitch in. Having this conversation when times are good may be a lot easier and a little less hostile than if you address the issue during tense times.

5. *Keep your bedroom up to par.* It's the room in the house that love built. Keep it orderly and attractive. Keep kindness and communication in and negativity out of this room for you and your mate. The benefits are immeasurable.

When things in a relationship are going poorly, it's imperative that each person tries to understand what's going wrong and to work toward fixing it. The same goes for working on a relationship when times are great. Care, connect, and be kind—even when you don't feel the *need* to.

My Homework Assignment for Chapter 6

1.

2.

3.

4.

5.

6.

Conclusion

Okay, godly women. You've heard me tell you about how good God is, and I've shared many stories. I'll leave you with this final one from my childhood. It's a great analogy of God's strength in your heart and home.

You know how it went with the Three Little Pigs. The first had a house of straw, the second a house of sticks, and the third a house of bricks. The big, bad wolf blew down the first two houses with a single huff and puff. The third pig's brick house held its own against the wolf's hot air. All of us have had—or will have—big, bad wolves that will try to blow our houses down. But God is in the bricks.

"The thief comes only to steal and kill and destroy; I came that they may have life, and have it abundantly" (John 10:10).

Let me share a time with you when a big, bad wolf came to my house. Here is my testimony, dear reader.

It was July 1992. We were preparing to go to Chicago to a relative's wedding. Before we could leave, my manager called me into his office to let me know that I had an important phone call from my doctor. I called my doctor back and received news that dropped the bottom out of my world: my biopsy had come back positive with the big C—cancer! *Why me?* I thought. I had to look to the Lord for consolation.

Help is available to us all; we just call on the Lord and ask for it. He is faithful to His Word. He will give us peace in the middle of our crises because we are putting our trust in Him.

"No temptation has overtaken you but such as is common to man; and God is faithful, who will not allow you to be tempted beyond what you are able, but with the temptation will provide the way of escape also, so that you will be able to endure it" (1 Corinthians 10:13).

I called my husband, and he came immediately to embrace me. He prayed with me and encouraged me from the Word of God. I felt much better, because I got a glimpse of God. I knew that my circumstances were not bigger than He was. So I began to see through the eyes of faith that God would help me to go through this sickness.

I began to read a book about prayer by a well-known author. I inserted my name everywhere it said "you" in Mark 11:24 (NKJV). "Therefore, I say to *you*, whatever things *you* ask when *you* pray, believe that *you* receive them, and *you* will have them." Then I left it up to the Holy Spirit and tried to enjoy the rest of the trip.

Three days later, we were on our way to San Antonio, Texas. The doctors in Dallas had set up everything I needed for the surgery. When I arrived, the tests began: X-rays, scans, blood work—you name it. The surgery was performed with no complications. I vividly remember the wonderful message that one of the oncologists gave me when I came to: "You are so, so lucky. But you know I don't believe in luck. God is in control, and everything came out okay."

On Sunday, my husband and I went to church at the hospital. I recall the chaplain's sermon on God's wisdom versus man's wisdom.

He said that God's wisdom is better than rubies or pearls, and there is nothing to be compared to it. You cannot learn godly wisdom in a university and get a degree in it. It can only come to a heart in a right relationship with God that is seeking it. The Holy Spirit that dwells within us leads us into all truth.

"I still have many things to say to you, but you cannot bear them now. However, when He, the Spirit of truth, has come, He will guide you into all truth; for He will not speak on His own authority, but whatever He hears He will speak; and He will tell you things to come. He will glorify me, for He will take of what is mine and declare it to you. All things that the Father has are mine. Therefore I said that

He will take of mine and declare it to you" (John 16:12–15 NKJV).

My husband and I prayed and cried, cried and prayed for my full recovery. I can't fully explain the feeling I experienced next, but I will try my best. A message came into the inner sanctuary of my heart. I heard these words so clearly: *Why subject yourself to chemotherapy and radiation? You don't need it!* I received two confirmations from my friends shortly afterward. A month later, I returned home—healed.

People came from the north, south, east, and west, bringing food, money, flowers, and prayers. People were praying for me all over the world. Thank God for the people of God! My dear friend Opal came immediately when she heard I had fallen ill and took excellent care of me. My dear son prepared breakfast for me every day. Praise God for children too!

During this time, God taught me many valuable lessons. One lesson was to trust Him completely. Another was that God is *much* bigger than any big, bad wolf. He is our protector and healer.

"'For I will restore health to you, and heal you of your wounds,' says the Lord, 'because they called you an outcast saying: "This is Zion; no one seeks her"'" (Jeremiah 30:17 NKJV).

"And let the peace of God rule in your hearts, to which also you were called in one body; and be thankful" (Colossians 3:15 NKJV).

I have been cancer-free for twenty years. Praise God for a godly husband and family. I shared this testimony to let you know that God will go before you and will never forsake you. He is your rock, solid and unmovable. Lean on Him, and He will never let you go. You might be saying to yourself, "I don't have a godly man who will pray for me. I don't even have a man." But God is there.

"The LORD is the one who goes ahead of you; He will be with you. He will not fail you or forsake you. Do not fear or be dismayed" (Deuteronomy 31:8).

God loves you, dear reader. He cares about you, your home, and every room of your house. His plan and His future for you don't alter because of your circumstances.

This is the time when he wants you to have that intimate relationship with Him. It's like water that has been infused with tea; you can't separate the tea from the water. Once Christ is infused into your very being, He their to stay. That is the greatest joy that we women have: knowing that we have an eternal relationship with God.

Confessions

Confession #1: A Godly Home

Father, I thank You that You have blessed me with all spiritual blessings in Christ Jesus.

Through skillful and godly wisdom in my life and my family, my home has been built.

Through Christ, my home is established on a sound and good foundation. Through knowledge, the chambers of every area shall be filled with all precious and pleasant riches—great priceless treasures. The house of the uncompromisingly righteous shall stand. Prosperity and welfare are in my house in the name of Jesus.

My house is securely built. It is founded upon a rock: revelation knowledge of Your Word, Father. Jesus is my cornerstone. Jesus is Lord of my household. Jesus is our Lord—Spirit, soul, and body.

Whatever may be our task, we work at it heartily as something done for You, Lord, and not for men. We love each other with a godly kind of love, and we dwell in peace. My home is deposited into your charge, entrusted to your protection and care.

Father, as for me and my house, we shall serve the Lord. In Jesus' name, amen!

Scriptures Readings

Ephesians 1:3

Proverbs 24:3–4

Proverbs 15:6

Psalm 112

Luke 6:4

Acts 4:1

Acts 16:31

Philippians 2:10–11

Colossians 3:23

Colossians 3:14

Joshua 24:1

Acts 20:3

Confession #2: Victorious Confessions for the Virtuous Woman

Father, I thank you that I am renewed in the spirit of my mind as I wait only upon you, for my hope and expectation are from You. I daily receive the manifestation of Your Word in my life, and I thank You, Father, that You have begun a good work in me and You will perform it until the day of Jesus Christ.

I am a capable, intelligent, virtuous woman.

I live the overcoming life.

I live in daily expectation of abundance for my life.

Every need in my life is met.

I have a sound mind.

I live a long life, because I am redeemed from the curse of the law.

I walk in divine health, and healing is my covenant right.

I am redeemed from the curse of the law. Because I dwell in the secret place of the Most High and abide under the shadow of the Almighty, "no plague comes nigh my dwelling."

The devourer is rebuked from my life and all that concerns me; he shall not destroy the fruit (children) of my ground; neither shall my vine cast its fruit before its appointed time, says the Lord of hosts.

He redeems my life from destruction; I overcome with my faith.

My mind is alert; my body is strong all the days of my life.

I live a life of purpose and fulfillment; I am a blessing to the kingdom of God.

Confession #3: Confession for the Unmarried State

Jesus Christ is Lord over my spirit, soul, and body. I am a child of God, loved by my Father. I live the victorious, overcoming life.

Every need in my life is met.

I choose to walk in the Spirit, and the lust of my flesh has no power over me. The Holy Spirit leads and guides me, for my steps are ordered by God.

God is preparing the perfect mate for me, and when the Spirit of God causes our paths to cross, I will have favor in his/her eyes. I choose to keep myself holy until marriage.

I walk in divine health; sickness and disease have no place in my body, because I am covered by the blood of Jesus.

I only think those things that are true, honest, pure, and of good report. I am committed to be diligent in the things of God, because God is a rewarder of the diligent.

I spend quality time helping others in the kingdom of God, and I am involved in my local church because this is the blessed state. In Jesus' name, I walk by faith and not by sight.

Confession #4: The Children

"Behold, children are a gift of the LORD. The fruit of the womb is a reward" (Psalm 127:3).

"Like arrows in the hand of a warrior, so are the children of one's youth. How blessed is the man whose quiver is full of them; they will not be ashamed when they speak with their enemies in the gate" (Psalm 127:4–5).

"All your sons will be taught of the LORD; and the well-being of your sons will be great" (Isaiah 54:13).

"And Jesus kept increasing in wisdom and stature, and in favor with God and men" (Luke 2:52).

"If you consent and obey; you will eat the best of the land" (Isaiah 1:19).

"Fathers, do not provoke your children to anger, but bring them up in the discipline and instruction of the Lord" (Ephesians 6:4).

"Children, obey your parents in the Lord, for this is right. Honor your father and mother (which is the first commandment with a promise), so that it may be well with you, and that you may live long on the earth" (Ephesians 6:1–3).

"The LORD will make you the head and not the tail, and you only will be above, and you will not be underneath, if you listen to the commandments of the LORD your God, which I charge you today, to observe them carefully" (Deuteronomy 28:13).

"Train up a child in the way he should go, even when he is old he will not depart from it" (Proverbs 22:6).

"May the LORD give you increase, you and your children. May you be blessed of the LORD, Maker of heaven and earth" (Psalm 115:14–15).

"Fathers, do not exasperate your children, so that they will not lose heart" (Colossians 3:21).

"They said, 'Believe in the Lord Jesus, and you will be saved, you and your household'" (Acts 16:31).

Appendix

The High Calling of Wife and Mother in Biblical Perspective

Is Homemaking a Challenging Career?

A career or professional pursuit requires training and preparation as well as commitment and dedication over the long haul; it demands consistent activity and progressive achievement; it is a combination of training and preparation, commitment and loyalty, energy and time, excellence and achievement. Finding an efficient, capable person who is professionally adequate in many and varied careers simultaneously is rare indeed. For example, would you want your family physician to be your postman and policeman as well? I doubt it. Why? Because you want him to specialize and sharpen his expertise in medicine. Yet, you are certainly aware that your doctor dictates letters and reports and that he may on occasion sit down with a troubled patient as counselor. Within most careers there is diversity of opportunity but never to the neglect of the priority responsibility. If the doctor gives the most productive part of his day to reports or counseling sessions and if, accordingly, he neglects updating his professional skills and treats patients haphazardly, the doctor will soon have no need to make reports or do counseling because his patient load will dwindle. In other words, there is specialization in purpose and preparation but generalization in service and opportunity.

Homemaking is a career. The dictionary defines the homemaker as "one who manages a household, especially a wife and mother." There are reasons why I believe this career is important enough to demand a woman's diligent preparation, foremost commitment, full energies, and greatest creativity. A homemaker does her job without the enticement of a paycheck, but she cannot be duplicated for any amount of money, for "She is worth far more than rubies" (Proverbs 31:10). Dorothy Morrison wrote, "Homemaking is not employment for slothful, unimaginative, incapable women. It has as much challenge and opportunity, success and failure, growth and expansion, perks and incentives, as any corporate career."[3]

Homemaking-A Divine Assignment

Keeping the home is God's assignment to the wife-even down to changing the sheets, doing the laundry, and scrubbing the floors. In <u>Titus 2:3-5</u>, Paul admonishes the older women to teach the younger women, among other things, "to love their husbands and children, to be busy at home" (oikourgous, Greek, literally "home-workers"). The home was once described as " ...a place apart, a walled garden, in which certain virtues too easily crushed by modern life could be preserved," and the mother in this home was described as "The Angel in the House."[4] A 1982 Gallup poll showed that more than eight out of ten respondents (82 percent) assigned top priority on an eleven-point scale to the importance of family life. Families, health, and self-respect all were rated as more important than the possession of material goods.[5]

Few women realize what great service they are doing for mankind and for the kingdom of Christ when they provide a shelter for the family and good mothering-the foundation on which all else is built. A mother builds something far more magnificent than any cathedral-the dwelling place for an immortal soul (both her child's fleshly tabernacle and his earthly abode). No professional pursuit so uniquely combines the most menial tasks with the most meaningful opportunities.

The Book of Proverbs is for me the most practical book in the Bible. No other book is more saturated with home and family and the relationships therein. No other book has any more to say to women specifically.

Proverbs 31 contains a full-length portrait of a godly heroine finished in minute detail. The passage is significant not only for what it includes but also for what it omits. There is no mention of rights or pursuit of self-serving interests; neither is the husband assigned to domestic pursuits. In fact, his occupation with other tasks is clearly stated, "Her husband has full confidence in her. ... Her husband is respected at the city gate, where he takes his seat among the elders of the land" (Proverbs 31:11, 23).

This beautiful and perfect ode of praise to womanhood is written as an acrostic with the first word of each verse beginning with one of the twenty-two successive letters of the Hebrew alphabet.

This description of God's "Bionic/Wonder Woman" is often labeled an "Alphabetic Ode," "The Golden ABC's of the Perfect Wife," "The Portrait of the Wife of Many Parts," "A Paradigm for Brides-to-Be." Perhaps its literary form is designed to make the passage easier to commit to memory, or its acrostic style may be a literary device used to emphasize that these characteristics describe God's ideal woman-committed homemaker, chaste helpmeet, upright and God-fearing woman of strength. Though no woman can match skills and creativity perfectly with this model, all can identify their respective talents within the composite, and all can strive for the spiritual excellence of this woman of strength. This passage is recited in many Jewish homes on the eve of Sabbath, not only setting the high challenge for wife and mother but also expressing gratitude for her awesome service to the household.[6]

At least half of <u>Proverbs 31:10-31</u> is occupied with personal and domestic energy. The New Testament, too, is clear in its emphasis on a woman's needed and necessary energy and efficiency in managing her household (<u>Titus 2:5</u>; <u>1Timothy 2:10</u>; <u>5:14</u>). When Jesus reprimanded Martha, He did not condemn the vital housework she was doing; neither did He decry the gracious hospitality extended to Himself (Jesus did not say *only* one thing is needful but pointed to the one thing Martha had omitted). He did admonish her not to be encumbered or burdened by her work to the exclusion of spiritual sustenance, which Mary had so faithfully sought (<u>Luke 10:38-42</u>). One is never to neglect spiritual preparation-not even for the joy of serving others.

The best way to make homemaking a joyous task is to offer it as unto the Lord; the only way to avoid the drudgery in such mundane tasks is to bathe the tasks with prayer and catch a vision of the divine challenge in making and nurturing a home. Brother Lawrence, a member of the barefoot Carmelite monks in Paris in the 1600s, set a worthy example: "Lord of all pots and pans and things ... Make me a saint by getting meals and washing up the plates!

The time of business does not with me differ from the time of prayer, and in the noise and clatter of my kitchen ...

I possess God in as great tranquility's if I were upon my knees at the Blessed Sacrament."

Many people are surprised to discover how much time it actually takes to run a household and care for a family.

Having a career was far easier for me than being a homemaker! None of my former positions required my being on the job twenty-four hours every day. None of my varied professional pursuits demanded such a variety of skills and abilities as I have exercised in homemaking. Automatic, labor-saving devices save much physical work, but increased mobility and multiplied outside activities add to the overall time demands so that the preparation and care of the family shelter are important enough for God Himself to assign that responsibility. Of course, much of the world would agree that being a housekeeper is acceptable as long as you are not caring for your own home; treating men with attentive devotion would also be right as long as the man is the boss in the office and not your husband; caring for children would even be deemed heroic service for which presidential awards could be given as long as the children are someone else's and not your own. We must not be overcome by the surrogacy of this age, which offers even a substitute womb for those so encumbered by lofty pursuits that they cannot accept God-given roles and assignments.

Homemaking-A Source of Self-Esteem

Women join men in the search for accomplishments and positive evaluations. We all have an innate desire to have worth. God's ideal woman has such worth. In fact, her worth cannot be fixed or estimated-it is "far more than rubies" (Proverbs 31:10). The question is, of course, clear: Who has such worth? The Hebrew word hayil, translated "virtuous" but more literally "strength,"[7] is found also in Proverbs 12:4; 31:29, and Ruth 3:11. It is further translated as *activity, ability, valor, wealth, efficiency, endurance, capability, energy.* This woman of strength enjoys dignity and importance in the administrative affairs of her home. She is a valuable helpmeet for her husband. She is a complement to her husband and a necessary completing part of his being.

There is beautiful reciprocity in this mutual relationship between husband and wife, just as there is between Christ and the church. Christ is the head of the church and the church is delighted to serve Him (Ephesians 5:23; Philippians 3:7-8). Christ finds joy in the church, and the church finds in Christ an inheritance of untold value. This husband has confidence in his wife's ability as the manager of the household affairs. She is absolutely dependable. The gain that accrues to her husband from her thrift and industry assures that he "lacks nothing of value" (Proverbs 31:11).

This "woman of strength" is a visionary investor. With her savings or inheritance, "She considers a field and buys it" (Proverbs 31:16). Unlike the unfaithful servant who hid the talent given to him by his master (Matthew 25:24-25), this prudent wife is continually adding to her husband's investments because "she plants a vineyard" (Proverbs 31:16).

The woman of strength is an elegant lady. Tapestry for bedding, carpeting, pillows was a sign of a carefully-decorated home interior. Silk cloth had not yet been invented, but she undoubtedly used the fine flax or linen cloth that was the best of the day, and purple garments, indicating wealth or high rank, which were rare indeed (Proverbs 31:22). God's woman does give time and effort to her appearance. These words were written about the wife of the great eighteenth-century preacher Jonathan Edwards,

But Sarah's husband made it clear that he treasured her as more than a housekeeping drudge and the mother of extra farmhands. So she stayed attractive, and fifteen years later she was still able to entrance men much younger than she was.[8]

The "woman of strength" was a source of tremendous pride to her husband. Her complete management of the household freed her husband to concentrate on his labors. Her husband respected her for neatness of dress, appreciated the fact that his wife was held in high esteem, and was willing to " …let her works bring her praise at the city gate" (Proverbs 31:31), but there is no hint in the passage that she had any other purpose than to meet the needs of her family in the best possible way.

Is Homemaking a Worthy Service?

In the Scriptures, the concern of godly women was not discrimination in vocation but rather the barrenness of the womb. Women were not pining away, pleading with the Almighty to be priests or prophets. They were praying for the blessing of bearing children. In Israel, every Jewish mother hoped to become the mother of the Messiah, who had been promised to Eve, the first mother (Genesis 3:15).

Hannah was brokenhearted over her childlessness (1 Samuel 1:1-2:1). Feeling forsaken of God, her maternal instinct prompted agonizing prayer with the burning intent of giving the boy back to God as a living sacrifice. Hannah deemed this the highest service. This motivation was not borne out of slavery to procreative responsibility. In conversations with her husband and Eli the priest, she was treated as an equal. The decision of when to go to Shiloh was left entirely with Hannah, and she not only was given the privilege of announcing the name of the child but also apparently chose the name Samuel, saying, "Because I asked the Lord for him" (1 Samuel 1:20, 22). Hannah was her own woman, but for her this meant committing herself to the purposes of God.

Hannah went from brokenhearted barrenness to extraordinarily privileged maternity. Though Hannah's psalm of thanksgiving marked her as a poetess and prophetess with a spiritual lyric equal to any psalm and full of theological truth, and though her words became the basis for Mary's Magnificent (Luke 1:46-55), Hannah did not reckon her literary acclaim equal to the nurturing of her child. Her greatest reward was not the birth of a son, however, but the gift to God of that son, who perhaps beyond all men had power with and from God. Moments of unequaled joy are coupled with difficult and time-consuming work. Children are not things to be acquired, used according to time and schedule, showcased for personal satisfaction, and then put aside for personal ambition and convenience.

Rearing the next generation is a coveted task despite the unprecedented attacks on motherhood. Some women want to limit parenthood to the labor room, settling for a "maternity sabbatical" in which they birth a baby during a few weeks' leave before rushing back to their lofty pursuits.

Mrs. Uyterlinde returned to her job as an executive secretary at an insurance company four months after the birth of her triplets, saying, "I could only do that with the help of two full-time housekeepers." She continued, "Working is easier than being at home, but I give them my total attention when I am at home. Luckily they don't all want it at the same time."[9]

Others opt to take parenthood a bit more seriously and thus choose the "mommy track" work plan so that their hours have some flexibility while the children are very young.[10] Still others depict motherhood as an awful condition, suffocating and degrading-psychic suicide. Their banner is "Motherhood-Just Say No!" God's warning through the prophet Ezekiel could not be more timely:

And you took your sons and daughters whom you bore to me and sacrificed them as food to the idols ... Everyone who quotes proverbs will quote this proverb about you: "Like mother, like daughter." You are a true daughter of your mother, who despised her husband and her children; and you are a true sister of your sisters, who despised their husbands and their children. (Ezekiel 16:20, 44-45).

Motherhood is both a demanding and a rewarding profession. Unfortunately, the reward often comes much later in life, but a prime characteristic of the good mother is unselfishness; she can wait for the final realization of her rewards. No one-not teacher, preacher, or psychologist-has the same opportunity to mold minds, nurture bodies, and develop potential usefulness like a mother. It is both practical and consistent with the basic qualities that nature has given male and female that the woman who bears and nurses the baby should care for the young and for the dwelling in which the young live. Though a woman approaching the twenty-first century is different in many ways from her foremothers, she is in at least one way forever the same. Some would say that she is a servant of her biological fate, to which she has to adjust her other pursuits. Of course, this may be interpreted as mere slavery with the procreative and nurturing tasks as the shackles; but, on the other hand, this biological duty may also be accepted as a divinely assigned destiny with the awesome opportunity for a woman to link hand and heart with the Creator God in bearing and preparing the next generation as the binding cord.

Despite pressures and difficulties, the job can be overwhelmingly satisfying and amazingly productive, because the result of really competent mothering will be passed from generation to generation. Products in the marketplace may come and go, but generation after generation we produce our sons and daughters. A child needs his mother to be all there; to be focused on him, to recognize his problems and needs; to support, guide, see, listen to him, love and want him. A young woman wrote to "Dear Abby" describing her mother as "a professional woman who collected a husband, a daughter, and a dog to enrich her life." According to the daughter, the only one not damaged by this enrichment was the dog![11] Susanna Wesley, the incomparably brilliant and well-educated mother of sons who shook two continents for Christ, wrote, "I am content to fill a little space if God be glorified." She described her now famous childrearing commitment in these words:

No one can, without renouncing the world, in the most literal sense, observe my method; and there are few, if any, that would entirely devote above twenty years of the prime of life in hopes to save the souls of their children, which they think may be saved without so much ado; for that was my principal intention, however unskillfully and unsuccessfully managed.[12]

The emergence of inexpensive, effective birth-control measures, not to mention widespread abortion, has cut the size of average families. Women are giving less and less of their time to childbearing and rearing; marriage is being delayed to allow career preparation and pursuit. Motherhood has become as mechanical and insignificant as any other household task and is just as quickly farmed out to others-even the carrying of the child in the womb, i.e., surrogate childbearing through in vitro fertilization.

Marriage has become such a partnership that the household tasks are carefully divided and assigned as nonchalantly as clients to be serviced. Both husband and wife choose careers according to the best earning power and opportunity for advancement of both, which usually means the family loses the best opportunity for both. Despite all this egalitarian emphasis, Mary Jo Bane of the Wellesley Women's Research Center expressed a prevailing sentiment: "Everybody is in favor of equal pay, but nobody is in favor of doing the dishes."[13]

Feminism is a "social movement" that demands it all. Actress Katharine Hepburn said in an interview, "I'm not sure any woman can successfully pursue a career and be a mother at the same time. The trouble with women today is that they want everything. But no one can have it all. I haven't been handicapped by children. Nor have I handicapped children by bringing them into the world and going ahead with my career."[14] Actress Joanne Woodward says, "My career has suffered because of the children, and my children have suffered because of my career. I've been torn and haven't been able to function fully in either arena. I don't know one person who does both successfully, and I know a lot of working mothers."[15] Golda Meir of Israel confessed that she suffered nagging doubts about the price her two children paid for her career, adding, "You can get used to anything if you have to, even to feeling perpetually guilty."[16]

Each of these women chose to work, not because she had to do so to provide necessities for her family or because her husband demanded it, but because of personal gain and fame or because of what she perceived to be a contribution more valuable to the nation or world than full-time motherhood. In each case, attention to the child was less important than the career.

Even the politicians are convinced that children are a valuable resource to be protected. A new report released by the National Governors' Association Task Force on Children states, "The economic and social well-being of the United States rests on our ability to assure that our children develop into healthy, well-educated, and productive citizens ... To invest in their future is to invest in ours."[17]

A study of primarily middle-class children was conducted by University of Texas at Dallas researchers Deborah Lowe Vandell and Mary Anne Corasaniti. This study indicated that full-time child care was associated with poorer study skills, lower grades, diminished self-esteem, and inadequate social interaction. Those who went into full-time care after the first year did not develop as well socially, emotionally, and intellectually as those in part-time care or those whose mothers stayed home with them. Surely another concern must be in the development of the child's values and worldview, which are determined very early in life.

Will forty hours a week in a day care center be a more formidable factor in forming those values than a worn-out mother? Because Vandell is a full-time professor and mother of three- and eight-year-old children, she had expected different results from the study. She clearly stated that she did not accept her findings as a call for mothers to stay at home.[18]

Napoleon was asked what could be done to restore the prestige of France. He replied, "Give us better mothers!"[19] The art of mothering surely demands as much training as a skilled waitress or craft worker, and thus we should not expect to be an expert as we begin this vocation but rather that slowly we would learn the needs of each child and how to meet those needs. Often those who are reluctant to begin the job of full-time mothering are just as reluctant to give it up when the results are both seen and enjoyed. Timothy Dwight, former president of Yale, said, "All that I am and all that I shall be I owe to my mother."[20] Good lives don't just grow like Topsy; they are built by people who care.

Isn't it amazing that legislators are looking for ways to enable families to send their children to day care rather than looking for ways to enable mothers to stay at home with their children? Megan Rosenfeld comments, "For the first time it is possible to envision a generation that will have spent the bulk of their childhood in an institution."[21] Sad but true is the fact that institutions are now set up to provide a substitute for the mother, who was the moral backbone and spiritual nurturer as well as the physical caretaker-the woman who is now no longer there!

Tatyana Zaslavskaya, president of the Soviet Sociologist Association, is quoted in a TASS interview as expressing deep concern for the ill effects on children of "the high rate of employment among working-age women." She pleaded for mothers to make children their prime mission, calling on the Communist Party to discuss ways to reduce the employment rate among mothers. She added that the problem that is often glamorized in the United States as the "Superwoman phenomenon (the woman who is faster than a speeding two-year-old, able to leap tall laundry piles in a single bound, and possessed of more power than three teenaged boys and still able to go out and save the world in the midst of all) has been known in the Soviet Union for years as "the problem of two jobs."[22] Even Mikhail Gorbachev addresses this issue:

We have discovered that many of our problems-in children's and young people's behavior, in our morals, culture and in production-are partially caused by the weakening of family ties and slack attitude to family responsibilities. This is a paradoxical result of our sincere desire to make women equal with men in everything.

He adds that Russia is now looking for ways to make it possible for women to return "to their purely womanly mission."[23]

Some women even claim to have a higher focus on serving God-putting the gospel ahead of "familyism."[24] While no one and nothing must come between a woman and her personal relationship to Christ ("But seek first his kingdom and his righteousness, and all these things will be given to you as well," Matthew 6:33), neither does the Bible contain any admonition to place the work of the church ahead of home responsibilities.

When a woman has chosen the high calling of being a wife, her submission to her husband is "as to the Lord" (Ephesians 5:22). When she chooses the high calling of motherhood, "Sons are a heritage from the Lord, children a reward from him" (Psalm 127:3); this, too, is itself an offering to the Lord.

In another era the beautiful and godly mother of John Chrysostom was widowed at a young age. She refused her many suitors and committed herself totally to the responsibility of rearing her gifted son, who became the Patristic church's greatest orator.[25] Mothers, too, win most by losing all ("Whoever finds his life will lose it, and whoever loses his life for my sake will find it," Matthew 10:39). By developing the Christ-like quality of abandoning personal demands and rights and seeking to serve and minister to those whom God has provided for their own personal ministry, these unselfish heroines gain worth and wonder and splendor beyond imagination.

There is no greater need for the coming years than a revival of interest in the responsibilities of motherhood.

We need mothers who are not only family-oriented but also family-obsessed. We have seen much about the virtue of determined childlessness and the right to make one's own place in the sun; yet it is hard to locate an aging mother who believes she made a mistake in pouring her life into her children, and it would certainly be more difficult to find a child to testify that his mother loved him and poured herself into his life to his detriment and demise. Surely countless mothers would join me in saying, "Try it-you'll like it!" The Lord Himself says, "Like arrows in the hands of a warrior are sons born in one's youth. Blessed is the man whose quiver is full of them" (Psalm 127:4-5).

Homemaking-An Opportunity for Service

The wife was created by God to be her husband's "helper" (ezer kenegdo, Hebrew, literally "a help like or corresponding to himself," Genesis 2:18). There is nothing demeaning about being a helper. It is a challenging and rewarding responsibility. God Himself assumed that role on many occasions (Psalm 40:17, "You are my help and my deliverer; O my God, do not delay"; Hebrews 13:6, "So we say with confidence, 'The Lord is my helper'"). This did not mean that the Lord was an inferior but spoke rather of His desire to meet the needs of those whom He loves with an everlasting and unconditional love.

Through the ages some have held that women are inferior to men, but the attempt to attribute such an idea to Scripture is unthinkable.

We must give attention to what Luther called "the plain sense of Scripture" as concerns the husband-wife relationship. It is really not terribly complicated. What the New Testament writers wrote and how they meant their words to be understood in their own time is far more important than the secular meanings assigned these Biblical terms in this generation, especially when those meanings depart from the clear teaching of Scripture. The fact is that there is no suggestion in Scripture that women are inferior or incapable in any sense-neither in personhood, which is the same as man's, nor in function, which is different from man's.

Any attitude or action suggesting a woman's insignificance, inferiority, or lack of personhood originated in the fall. The stigma of inferiority is no more appropriate for the wife than it would be for Christ. One can be subject to a superior as Israel was subject to the Lord (Deuteronomy 6:1-5) and as believers are subject to Christ (Philippians 2:9-11), or as Abraham submitted to the priesthood of Melchizedek (Hebrews 7:7).

But subordination is also possible among equals: Christ is equal to God the Father and yet subject to Him (Philippians 2:6-8); believers are equal to one another and yet are admonished to "submit to one another out of reverence for Christ" (Ephesians 5:21). In fact, one can be called to subordinate himself to someone who is inferior, as Christ submitted to Pontius Pilate, making "no reply, not even to a single charge" (Matthew 27:11-14). The mere fact that wives are told to be subject to their husbands tells us nothing about their status. It is the comparison of the relationship between husband and wife to the relationship of God the Father with God the Son that settles the matter of status forever.[26]

Submission and *authority*, which to the feminists are the offensive elements in Biblical womanhood, are not terms that in themselves connote sinful or evil characteristics. Neither are the terms limited to describe role relationships between the sexes. Both terms are used to describe relationships within the family, including, but not exclusive to, the relationship between husband and wife. In fact, these terms even reach far beyond the family. In every facet of organized society (see Romans 13:1-5 for application to government and Hebrews 13:17 as concerns the church), there must be both authority and submission to authority; otherwise, there is anarchy. There simply is no justification for labeling these words and the concepts they embody as innately objectionable and oppressive. Finally, and more importantly, these terms point to our common ground with the Lord Himself, who gave to us the highest example of servant hood, obedience, and selflessness, as "he humbled himself and became obedient to death" (Philippians 2:5-8; see also John 5:30).

Ideally, the care of one's partner is inherent in marriage. Each makes an active and unique (not passive and same) contribution to the marriage, and each depends upon the other for that contribution. Both husband and wife achieve their respective individuality by assuming different roles, for which each is needed and on which neither intrudes. In choosing to allow one's husband to support the family, a wife can turn her ingenuity toward producing a lifestyle even better than an additional salary would buy.

Subordination has been distorted before in the history of the church. Arius assigned inferiority of being to Jesus the Son, refusing to accept the Scripture's statement that Father, Son, and Holy Spirit are equal in being and personhood (John 1:1; 5:23; 10:30; 14:6-7, 9, 11) and yet different in office and function, as the Son voluntarily becomes subject and even subordinate[27] to the Father (John 5:19-20; 6:38; 8:28-29, 54; 1 Corinthians 15:28; Philippians 2:5-11), and the Holy Spirit is sent by, and thus under the direction of, the Father to glorify the Son (John 14:26; 15:26; 16:13-14). Arian subordinationism was condemned as heretical-a denial of Trinitarianism-because it ignored, distorted, or misread certain Scriptures and because of Gnostic tendencies that simply dismissed or abandoned passages that the human mind could not explain.[28] Can "Arian" feminism, which denies that women can have equal personhood along with a subordinate role, i.e., a different role with equal worth, be any more circumspect? I certainly think not. The Council of Nicea in a.d. 325 not only condemned this heresy but also ascribed to both Son and Spirit an equality of being, while clearly declaring subordination of order and function.[29] Likewise, I have no problem in accepting within my womanhood the equality of creation and personhood, while recognizing that my divinely bestowed womanhood is uniquely suited to the divinely assigned task.

Too many women rush headlong into a career outside the home, determined to waste no time or effort on housework or baby-sitting but rather seeking to achieve position and means by directing all talents and energies toward non-home professional pursuits. It is true that many "perfect jobs" may come and go during the childrearing years, but only one will absolutely never come along again-the job of rearing your own children and allowing them the increasingly rare opportunity to grow up at home.

Golda Meir, by her own testimony, devoted her adult life to the birth and rearing of Israel at the cost of her marriage. She separated from her reticent husband in pursuit of public life. To quote Mrs. Meir, "what I was made it impossible for him to have the sort of wife he wanted and needed ... I had to decide which came first: my duty to my husband, my home and my child or the kind of life I myself really wanted. Not for the first time-and certainly not for the last-I realized that in a conflict between my duty and my innermost desires, it was my duty that had the prior claim."[30]

How sad it is for a woman to try to build her life on the notion that she is going to pursue whatever momentarily happens to gratify her needs socially, emotionally, physically, or professionally. Though the duty of wifehood and motherhood may lay claim, the desires of personal ambition and success in public service can take hold, of which the Lord warned, but each one is tempted when, by his own evil desire [epithumia, Greek], he is dragged away and enticed. Then, after desire has conceived, it gives birth to sin [hamartia, Greek, literally "missing the mark"]; and sin, when it is full grown, gives birth to death. (James 1:14-15)

When a wife goes to work outside the home, often her husband and children go through culture shock. Suddenly the husband has added to his vocational work increased family assignments. He is frustrated over the increase in his own assignments and guilty over his wife's increased fatigue and extended hours to keep up at home. God did give the husband the responsibility of providing for the family (Genesis 2:15). To sabotage his meeting that responsibility is often a debilitating blow to the man personally and to the marriage. A woman's career can easily serve as a surrogate husband, as during employment hours she is ruled by her employer's preferences. Because the wife loses much of her flexibility with the receipt of a paycheck, a husband must bend and adapt his schedule for emergencies with the children, visits to the home by repairmen, etc.

This leaves two employers without totally committed employees and children without a primary caretaker utterly devoted to their personal needs and nurturing. Note the prophet's warning, "Youths oppress my people, women rule over them. O my people, your guides lead you astray; they turn you from the path" (Isaiah 3:12).

Many women still see the paycheck as an inadequate trade for the sights and sounds and tastes of home. Though some see their paychecks as representing independence and achievement, to be bound to paychecks requires in exchange the time formerly allotted to work for the family in private, personal ways. This is not to say that there are never times when a woman should seek employment outside her home. Nevertheless, are we coming to a day when a woman's employment outside the home is the rule rather than the exception, leaving no one to give primary attention to the home and to producing the next generation.

The most outstanding ministering couple in the New Testament is the dynamic duo Aquila and Priscilla, who traveled the apostolic world together, sharing the gospel of Christ and expounding the Word more fully (Acts 18:2-3, 18, 26). Priscilla must have been a diligent and discerning student of the Word of God, or she could never have impressed the learned Apollos. On the other hand, she must have been a gracious hostess to have endeared her home and hospitality to Paul. Obviously, she was encouraged to take an active part in ministry by her husband. When a godly wife is all she ought to be, she completes, complements, and extends her husband. Their joint ministry reaches beyond what either of them could do alone (Psalm 34:3; Ecclesiastes 4:9-12).

When Paige Patterson invited me to link my life to his, irrevocably and inseparably, he asked me to join him in study and preparation. How grateful I have been for the formal studies of seminary, but how much more grateful I am for the hours Paige has spent as my teacher and mentor. Paige has encouraged me in multifarious ministry, but never has he given me the impression that these ministries were to be more important than keeping our home and rearing our children. (Dorothy Patterson, The High Calling of Wife and Mother in Biblical Perspective, Copyright year 1996-2006], Biblical Studies Press; reprinted with permission from http://bible.org

Conclusion

D espite the clear positive principles and the precise warnings of consequences for those who ignore or distort God's plan for the home and family, we find ourselves living in the very "upside-down" world the prophet Isaiah described:

You turn things upside down, as if the potter were thought to be like the clay! Shall what is formed say to him who formed it, "He did not make me"? Can the pot say of the potter, "He knows nothing"? (Isaiah 29:16).

The efforts of contemporary society to eradicate the differences between the sexes have spawned an increase in strident lesbianism and open homosexuality, a quantum upward leap in divorces, an increase in rapes and sexual crimes of all sorts-and families smaller in size than ever before. We are part of a generation of women who have prostituted the creative purposes of God by prophesying "out of their own imagination" (Ezekiel 13:17), who have erected for themselves "male idols" to supplant the Creator's design (Ezekiel 16:17), and who have cast aside the greatest blessing of the Creator, i.e., the fruit of the womb (Ezekiel 16:20, 44-45). We have allowed Scripture itself to be distorted so that we are conforming ourselves to this age and letting the world squeeze us "into its own mold" (Romans 12:2, *Phillips*). The church today sounds like the world twenty-five years ago; it has lost its great power to stand against culture. Scripture has been shanghaied to suit the purposes of the age and to conform to the current cultural scene. The virtues and vices of Christianity have been inverted so that self-gratifying personal rights, selfishness, and self-interests are exalted, whereas self-effacing submission, humility, and service to others are degraded. While I am not implying that every career woman is selfish, I am saying that the social atmosphere that causes women to crave professional pursuits over the family is perverted by unbiblical assumptions and an ungodly spirit of assertion and self-gratification.

Evangelical or Biblical feminism is in large measure a product of the secular women's liberation movement of the late sixties and seventies. Few of these evangelical feminists have much in common with the radical wing of feminism. Nevertheless, the movement of self-assertion in the home, church, and community cannot but extend into the spiritual realm with a determination to act independently of God and go one's own way (Proverbs 14:12; Isaiah 53:6). Human rights and reason have been exalted over responsibility and divine revelation. The reality in Scripture has been subordinated to the reason of man (and woman); the absolutes of the Creator have been replaced with the whims of the creation. Rejecting Scripture as authoritative, many male and female feminists put the focus of authority in human hands, usually through some hermeneutical casuistry. Whatever texts do not seem to affirm women are labeled as not authoritative, while texts judged as affirming are authoritative.

There is great resistance in the world of feminism to letting Scripture speak for itself. Instead of coming reverently to the Biblical text to see what it says and then declaring themselves to be feminists, many seem to have found something in secular feminism and in its claims for improving the lot of womanhood that seemed good and true to them. Thus, the feminists took a "leap of faith" to attach themselves to this movement, determining to legitimize their position Biblically and theologically and to change two millennia of church history and tradition to reflect this new church doctrine that more nearly fits the reality of their active professional lives-another tragic example of the world's setting the agenda for the church rather than vice versa.

Homemaking, if pursued with energy, imagination, and skills, has as much challenge and opportunity, success and failure, growth and expansion, perks and incentives as any corporation, plus something no other position offers-working for people you love most and want to please the most!

In the words of Scripture, I have found a worthy challenge:

Teach them [God's words] to your children, talking about them when you sit at home and when you walk along the road, when you lie down and when you get up ... so that your days and the days of your children may be many in the land that the Lord swore to give your forefathers, as many as the days that the heavens are above the earth. (Deuteronomy 11:19, 21)

Homemaking-being a full-time wife and mother-is not a destructive drought of usefulness but an overflowing oasis of opportunity; it is not a dreary cell to contain one's talents and skills but a brilliant catalyst to channel creativity and energies into meaningful work; it is not a rope for binding one's productivity in the marketplace, but reins for guiding one's posterity in the home; it is not oppressive restraint of intellectual prowess for the community, but a release of wise instruction to your own household; it is not the bitter assignment of inferiority to your person, but the bright assurance of the ingenuity of God's plan for complementarity of the sexes, especially as worked out in God's plan for marriage; it is neither limitation of gifts available nor stinginess in distributing the benefits of those gifts, but rather the multiplication of a mother's legacy to the generations to come and the generous bestowal of all God meant a mother to give to those He entrusted to her care.

[1] All Scripture quoted will be from the *New International Version* unless otherwise specified.

[2] Frank Zepezauer, "The Masks of Feminism," *The Human Life Review*, Fall 1988, p. 31.

[3] My Turn, *Newsweek*, October 17, 1988, p. 14.

[4] Paul Fussell, "What Happened to Mother?" *The Wilson Quarterly*, vol. xii, no. 5 (Winter 1988), p. 154.

[5] George Gallup, "Intangibles Rated Highest by Americans," *The Dallas Morning News*, January 28, 1982, p. 24D.

[6] Hymen E. Goldin, *The Jewish Woman and Her Home* (New York: Hebrew Publishing Co., n.d.), pp. 130-131.

[7] Francis Brown, S.R. Driver, and Charles Briggs, *A Hebrew and English Lexicon of the Old Testament* (Oxford: Clarendon Press, 1962), pp. 298-299.

[8] Elizabeth Dodds, *Marriage to a Difficult Man* (Philadelphia: Westminster Press, 1976), p. 84.

[9] *The Dallas Morning News*, September 22, 1981.

[10] *The Dallas Morning News*, March 11, 1989.

[11] Abigail Van Buren, "Dear Abby," *The Northwest Arkansas Times*, September 28, 1974.

[12] Rebecca Lamar Harmon, Susanna, *Mother of the Wesleys* (London: Hodder Stoughton, 1968), p. 57.

[13] *San Francisco Examiner*, December 28, 1977.

[14] "An Interview with Kate Hepburn," *Ladies Home Journal*, March, 1977, p. 54.

[15] "Joanne and Paul," *Ladies Home Journal*, July, 1975, p. 62.

[16] "Books," *Newsweek*, November 3, 1975, p. 88.

[17] Kim A. Lawton, "Politicians Discover Children," *Christianity Today*, March 17, 1989, p. 34.